KT-482-724

The Shadow of the Tower

Joan Macalpine

The Shadow of the Tower

Henry VII and his England,
background to the BBC tv series

British Broadcasting Corporation

Published by the British Broadcasting Corporation,
35 Marylebone High Street, London W1M 4AA

ISBN 0 563 10503 8

First published 1971

Printed in England by Cox & Wyman Ltd,
London, Reading and Fakenham

Contents

1 Henry's England   7
2 The Fugitive Prince   10
3 King of England   14
4 The Dark Earl   21
5 Interlude with Heresy   30
6 The French Lad   35
7 A Fly in the Ointment   42
8 The New Found Land   46
9 The Cornish Rising   52
10 End of a Pretender   58
11 Master in his House   70
12 The Last Pretender   78
13 To End Alone   88
    Family Tree   96
    Chronology   98

Acknowledgements

Acknowledgement is due to the following for permission
to reproduce the illustrations between pp. 52–3:
plate 1 Radio Times Hulton Picture Library; 2 Eric de Maré;
3, 5 National Portrait Gallery; 4 W. Eaden Lilley & Co.
Ltd; 6 (top) Kunsthistorisches Museum, Vienna;
6 (bottom) Mansell Collection; 7 Edwin Smith; 8 Public
Record Office, London. The maps were drawn by
David Jefferis.

1 Henry's England

The England whose crown rolled into a thorn-bush at Bosworth Field was a green and fertile land, well worth fighting for. The midlands and the south were for the most part a rolling forest of oak-trees beyond which, to the north, west and east, stretched hill, moorland and fens. Here and there, in a clearing, a sheltered valley or a raised patch in the fens, there would be a village, a hamlet or a group of farms. In places the woods had been cleared – by the Sussex ironmasters or by the sheep which brought the country its trading wealth.

Through the woods and over the hills and moors wound trackways, rutted or muddy in summer and almost impassable in winter, with a few straight, firm roads to remind scholars that the Romans once ruled the land. Rivers were the important highways, the only ones not impassable in bad weather. It was a land where remote counties were almost beyond the King's reach, and where only rumour travelled quickly.

The people – between three and four million of them – were still marked by great differences in regional types. Men of the north-east were as much as two inches taller than those of the south-west, and easterners were fairer than midlanders. Each region had its dialect, incomprehensible to outsiders. They were a turbulent, unruly race, who admitted that 'the French vice is lechery and the English vice treachery'. Every time Parliament voted taxes to Henry VII there was an uprising somewhere, and a tax-gatherer's life tended to be a short one. The Duke of Northumberland, reconciled to Henry after Bosworth, lost his life four years later, trying to argue with a mob demonstrating against him as he collected the King's taxes.

Such mobs recruited their strength by eating enormously – one foreigner noted that 'though they live in hovels, they eat like lords' – and by being careful not to overwork – 'it is received as a prescript that they should sweat by no means'. Their unruliness was made the more dangerous by the law which required every able-bodied man to have weapons ready for use in an emergency – weapons which were often turned against the King's officers.

The gentry, living on their own land, had a great longing for order, and Henry made them his chief arm of government. Their lives were spent in hunting their woods, farming their land, ordering their parishes, suing their neighbours and punishing petty criminals. Of an evening they might dream of a return of the past, golden age – *Morte d'Arthur* was published in 1485, and was written by Sir Thomas Malory 'that we fall not through vice and sin, but exercise and follow virtue' while he was in prison for robbery with violence, attempted murder, sacrilege, extortion and rape.

One man in ten lived in a town – most of them overgrown villages in our eyes. Even from the centre of London it was an easy walk to the fields, which was just as well, for the houses in towns were close-packed, with a pig and a few hens in each backyard and almost no sanitation. Instead of employing dustmen, London relied on scavenging rooks, ravens and jackdaws.

It was one of the great cities of Europe, with a population of about 75,000 crowded within its walls and spilling out beyond them. To the east, dominating the city, stood the great, dark Tower – a palace, a prison and a maze of offices and store-rooms. There was the royal menagerie, where Londoners could bring their children to see the lions and leopards. There was the Mint and there, for a time, was the royal alchemist seeking the perfect solution to taxation problems.

Between the Tower and Westminster the great highway was the Thames – wider than it is now and spanned by a single bridge which was one of the wonders of the world. Flocks of swans and other water-birds threaded their way among flocks of boats carrying goods and people to and fro, from one landing to another, and on upstream to Staines, Maidenhead and Oxford, or downstream to meet the ships which sailed to all the countries of Europe.

The royal family moved constantly from one palace or manor to another, chiefly in London and the home counties, but moving much further in the summer. There were royal palaces at the Tower of London, Baynard's Castle (just south of St Paul's Cathedral), Westminster, Greenwich, Windsor and Sheen (rebuilt as

Richmond when it burned down in 1498) and numerous royal manor houses in small towns like Esher and Eltham (where the royal nursery was). A summer progress could range north to Newcastle, west to Taunton, south to the Isle of Wight or east to Norwich, spending some days in royal houses and some in the large houses of prosperous members of the nobility, gentry and episcopacy. Wherever the King went, the administration went too – a Whitehall on wheels – so that he spent more than £1,000 a month on feeding about 700 people a day. In those numbers lies the reason for the royal restlessness. The King's entourage would literally eat itself out of house and home, foul what little drainage there was and move on, leaving the resident servants to 'sweeten' the building again and re-establish food supplies.

On his first great move, riding through London to take possession of the Tower after Bosworth, Henry was – shakily – King of a weak and divided country on the edge of the world. South and east, over the water, lay the Great Powers – France, Spain and the Empire. By 1492, when Anne of Brittany married Charles VIII of France, the whole south channel coast, from Brest to Boulogne, was in the hands of a powerful and potentially hostile King. The danger was real: ships of the period had great difficulty in sailing into the wind, and southern England was, for most of the year, a lee shore, easy to attack and difficult to defend. The country was open to invasion along the whole of its south coast and also from Ireland (where Henry had almost no power) and from Scotland (France's old ally). Henry might well have had to face a concerted attack from all three directions. It was lucky for him that Charles VIII had his eyes on Italy and only half a mind for fomenting trouble in vulnerable England, or for seizing the more solid and accessible wealth of the Netherlands, whose trade in wool and cloth was England's chief source of foreign revenue.

2 The Fugitive Prince

Henry Tudor's father was Edmund, son by a secret marriage of Katherine de Valois, widow of Henry V, and Owen Tudor, clerk of her wardrobe. His mother, who was not quite fourteen years old when he was born, was Margaret Beaufort, great-granddaughter of John of Gaunt and his mistress, Katherine Swynford. It was a family which moved in the highest ranks of royal bastardy.

The child born in Pembroke castle in 1457 was no claimant to the throne – it was only as other leaders died that Lancastrians began to turn their minds to him. In the meantime he had a turbulent and insecure childhood. His father died before he was born and when he was four years old his grandfather was executed by the Yorkists and his uncle, Jasper Tudor, fled to Scotland as Edward of York proclaimed himself King Edward IV. Henry was put in the charge of a Yorkist noble. It was no strict imprisonment, however: his mother's second marriage, to Lord Stafford, eldest son of the Duke of Buckingham, gave her a foot in the Yorkist camp and she quickly established an ascendancy over his guardian. It is difficult to find anyone in Margaret Beaufort's life over whom she did not establish an ascendancy.

The fortune of war brought Henry VI briefly back to the throne in 1470 and Uncle Jasper presented his nephew at court. But within a year Edward IV was back, Henry VI and his son were dead, and Jasper was fleeing to Brittany, taking Henry Tudor with him. So many royal deaths had increased the boy's importance, and Edward IV asked the Duke of Brittany to send him to London, saying that he wanted him to marry his daughter, Princess Elizabeth. The Duke handed Henry over to the English ambassadors and he set out on a journey which he must have known would end in the Tower. But at the last moment the Duke changed his mind. His treasurer caught the English ambassadors up at St Malo and asked them to hand over their prisoner. They protested vehemently and while the treasurer argued with them his soldiers sneaked the prisoner away to sanctuary, and from there to semi-captivity at the court of Brittany.

Meanwhile Margaret Beaufort's second husband died and she married Thomas, Lord Stanley, one of the great men at the Yorkist court – great enough to become Princess Elizabeth's guardian when Edward IV died. And when Richard of Gloucester became King Richard III, Stanley (after weekending in the Tower) became Constable of England, his wife carrying the Queen's train at the coronation and gently insisting on precedence not only over her fellow countesses, but also over the duchesses of Suffolk and Buckingham.

John Morton, the sixty-year-old bishop of Ely, was a suspected Lancastrian in the custody of the Duke of Buckingham – the man who had chiefly helped Richard to the throne and who had been the father of Margaret Beaufort's second husband. Buckingham soon began to feel that Richard was ungrateful to him, and between Margaret Beaufort and John Morton his discontent did not lack guidance. He decided to support Henry.

The Queen Dowager – widow of Edward IV – would be a critical figure in any conspiracy because of the importance of her eldest daughter, Elizabeth of York. She was a tempestuous, difficult woman who managed to get herself disliked by almost everyone she had dealings with. When Richard III had seized power she had taken sanctuary at Westminster, breaking down part of a wall between the palace and the monastery so that her furniture could take sanctuary with her, and there she now was, closely watched and seething with discontent. A Welsh doctor slipped unchallenged past her guards and she agreed that Princess Elizabeth should marry Henry Tudor if he defeated Richard III. Margaret Beaufort's steward, Reginald Bray, travelled the country, discreetly visiting other malcontents, and messengers slipped quietly over to Brittany.

It was decided that Henry should invade Wales on 18 October 1483, and that on the same day there should be risings at Brecknock, Exeter, Salisbury and Maidstone. It was an act of optimism to hope to synchronise risings in those days of poor communications and the conspirators were defeated by Richard's skill and energy and by the English weather – a storm scattered Henry's ships and bogged down the risings in torrential rain. Buckingham was executed. Margaret Beaufort was committed to the custody of her husband. Morton escaped to the low countries. Other fugitives, including the Marquis of Dorset, the Queen Dowager's son by her first marriage to Sir John Grey, joined Henry, forming a little court in exile around a Pretender to the throne.

On Christmas Day 1483, in Rennes cathedral, this Pretender stood before his court, a tall, thin young man, twenty-seven years old, with fair hair, a fair complexion, a friendly smile and an alert, wary disposition. He proclaimed himself King Henry VII of England, accepted their oaths of allegiance, and promised to marry Princess Elizabeth as soon as he had secured his crown.

A messenger from Morton warned Henry that Richard was prospering in negotiations with Brittany, and Henry asked France if he could take refuge there. Then, disguised as a page, he rode for the frontier, his pursuers only an hour behind him. One by one, his little court followed, and in France they were joined by their latest, most valuable recruit. John de Vere, thirteenth Earl of Oxford, had spent his life in the wars. His father and elder brother had been executed by the Yorkists in 1462, when he was twenty. He had submitted to Edward IV and been treated well by him, but when Warwick the Kingmaker took up the Lancastrian cause Oxford changed sides with him and fought with him at the disastrous battle of Barnet, where Warwick was killed. He seized St Michael's Mount in Cornwall, and held it through a long siege which ended in his surrendering on condition that no member of the garrison should lose his life. He was attainted, which meant that his estates were forfeit to the crown – though his wife was given an annuity of £100 a year – and Richard III sent him as a prisoner to the castle of Hammes in the Pas de Calais, the last remnant of England's French territory. He and his jailer, James Blount, commander of the castle, got to talking together, and eventually jailer and prisoner together rode out of Hammes to join Henry. In the Earl of Oxford and Uncle Jasper, Henry had two seasoned soldiers to lead his army.

England's weakness and division was France's strength, so the French government lent him 60,000 francs and 1,800 mercenaries – described in one French account as the worst rabble one could find. But he was in no position to be choosy: Richard was in touch with some of his supporters. Already the Queen Dowager had told Dorset that she was reconciled, and if he would come home all would be forgiven. He tried to slip away. Henry had him brought back and, when the French asked for some security against their loan, left him behind, in pawn in Paris. But Henry had to move quickly, before more loyalties wavered. South Wales was dominated by Rhys ap Thomas, a member of the gentry who had spent his adolescence at the court of Philip of Burgundy, and returned home to organise his tenants and neighbours into a potential fighting force of several thousand. Richard III gave him an annuity of forty marks a year, but early in 1485 he made contact with Henry, who hoped that he would bring his part of the country to support a Welsh King. He looked to the Stanleys (dominated by his mother) to bring in the northern Welsh. He knew that Richard was expecting him, waiting with a seasoned army in a central headquarters at Nottingham and watching the coasts, but he could not afford to put off his attempt. He embarked his tiny army in six ships and sailed for Milford Haven on the wild and unwatchable coast of Pembrokeshire.

3 King of England

Henry landed on 7 August 1485, kneeling down at once to sing 'Judica me, Deus, et decerna causam meam', and marched east to Shrewsbury, where Rhys ap Thomas joined him. The Welsh had been shocked by rumours of the murder of the little princes in the Tower and the reputation of Jasper Tudor stood high – there were prophecies that 'Jasper will breed for us a dragon – he is the hope of our race'. On the whole they sympathised with Henry, but they did not rush unanimously to support him.

He marched from Shrewsbury along Watling Street, turning a little aside to pause at Tamworth, where he was joined by some deserters from Richard who reported that he had a strong and well-disciplined army. Henry paused to confer with them and so got separated from his own army, which he had sent on to Tamworth. All night he wandered, almost alone and unable to ask for help. Next day, when he found his men, he explained away his disappearance by saying that he had been on an excursion to contact secret supporters.

Tamworth castle yielded him its cannon, which slowed his advance but proved invaluable in the coming battle. Then, in the dawn of 20 August, the Stanley brothers came secretly to meet him. They brought cold comfort: Lord Stanley, Margaret Beaufort's husband, could not join him because Richard was holding his son, Lord Strange, hostage. Sir William Stanley, with no such good reason, was non-committal: he seems to have had an ingrained need to butter his bread on both sides. The Stanleys rode away and Henry swung his force of about 5,000 men off Watling Street to meet Richard's 10,000 as they marched from Leicester through Market Bosworth towards him. It was open country, much of it bare moorland and fen. Ambien Hill was probably treeless and commanded the flattish land about it. The positions of the various forces in the battle are debatable – what follows is the most likely account of the day.

Sir William Stanley rejoined his men, camped to the north of

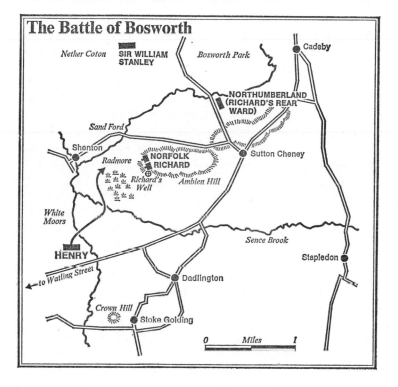

The Battle of Bosworth

Nether Coton   **SIR WILLIAM STANLEY**   *Bosworth Park*   ● Cadeby

NORTHUMBERLAND (RICHARD'S REAR WARD)

Sand Ford

● Shenton

Radmore   **NORFOLK RICHARD**   ● Sutton Cheney

Richard's Well   *Ambien Hill*

White Moors

HENRY   *Sence Brook*   ● Stapledon

← *to Watling Street*

● Dadlington

Crown Hill ● Stoke Golding

0   *Miles*   1

Ambien Hill. Lord Stanley's men were between Henry and Richard and he fell back before Henry's advance, as if to join Richard. On the night of Sunday 21 August the armies were within striking distance of each other. Henry's camp was on the White Moors, south of Shenton. Richard was at Sutton Cheney, with his rear ward – under Northumberland – about half a mile to the north, within sight of Sir William Stanley. Lord Stanley was probably near Stapledon, where he could be in touch with both Richard and Henry.

It was high summer and both armies were on the move by six o'clock next morning. Richard's fore ward under Norfolk and his main ward, commanded by himself, occupied Ambien Hill, where he is said to have drunk from the spring called Richard's Well as he watched Henry advance to Radmore (the Red Moor), his flanks protected by the brook and the marsh on either side. Henry sent to Lord Stanley, asking him to advance, and received an ambiguous reply which must have filled him with dread. Even with its cannon (Richard's cannon had not arrived in time) his army had little chance without the Stanleys, and none at all if they fought at Richard's side.

Richard had even greater cause for concern. He commanded both Northumberland and Lord Stanley to join him. Northumberland made no reply and took no action – he and Sir William Stanley stood still and watched each other. Lord Stanley at last committed himself, sent Richard a flat refusal, and advanced towards the gap between the marsh and the hill.

Richard, watching the slow advance and deployment of Henry's men, hampered by their cannon, the softness of the ground and the narrowness of the corridor between the marsh and the stream, realised that he must win quickly or not at all – the action must be decided before Lord Stanley could join battle. He launched and led a wild charge, directing his men towards Henry's main ward and Henry himself, whose death would instantly decide the issue. He personally killed Henry's standard-bearer, threw down another man and attacked Henry, who kept him at bay until help came. Lord Stanley's men, threatening to encircle him, forced Richard to retreat.

He was killed, probably near the Sand Ford. At this point Sir

William Stanley, seeing that Northumberland was making no move, joined the battle, and Richard's men were driven south over the lower slopes of Ambien Hill to Dadlington and beyond. Near Stoke Golding Henry's men halted and gathered to acclaim their new King. Tradition has it that Richard's crown was found in a thorn bush and set on Henry's head as he stood on Crown Hill. The day had been won by Henry's cannon, Northumberland's inactivity and the intervention of first one and then the other of the Stanley brothers.

Having given thanks to God for the victory, Henry knighted eleven of his followers (one of them was Rhys ap Thomas – who never rose to a higher rank, though he was throughout the reign one of the great men of Wales, a member of the Council and called 'father Rhys' by the King himself). Then he set off for London, sending Sir Robert Willoughby to Sheriff Hutton castle in Yorkshire, where Richard had lodged Princess Elizabeth and his ten-year-old nephew, the Earl of Warwick. With Richard dead the Yorkists might turn to Warwick, the next male in the line of succession, or to the Earl of Lincoln, who had been named by Richard as his heir. Lincoln had fought in the battle and disappeared: he must be found and Warwick secured in the Tower at once.

London met Henry with the fullest honours, as it had each successive King through the Wars of the Roses. After a nasty delay while the sweating sickness killed two successive mayors, six aldermen and countless citizens, everyone turned out to cheer jubilantly as their new, mysterious King from nowhere rode through their streets from the Tower to Westminster for the coronation. It was a magnificent display, calculated to create the impression that this King – who had financed his invasion by pawning the Marquis of Dorset – was a wealthy, powerful and secure monarch.

Henry dealt with the weakness of his claim to the throne by never trying to prove it. He simply proclaimed himself King, tracing his descent from Cadwallader, a hero too remote and legendary for argument. He laid stress on the distance between himself and any subject, however great (a wise precaution, after the 'kingmaking' nobles of the past few generations). The word 'majesty' entered the language to describe him. Even at first, when he was in debt, he wore magnificent clothes and jewels. When he ate he was served by nobles. He established the Yeomen of the Guard (the first standing army in English history – but there were only about 150 of them). In public he moved under a canopy of state, surrounded by ceremonial. His love of jewels (in twelve years he spent more than £100,000 on them) may have sprung originally from their being readily portable if ever he had to leave in a hurry.

His little court-in-exile formed the nucleus of his Council. Morton came home to become Archbishop of Canterbury and Chancellor of England, bringing the support of the church and the pope to his aid. The pope confirmed Bosworth by recognising Henry as King and any future opponents as rebels to be excommunicated. The church in England provided the Civil Service – the administrators and clerks – and their loyal service was vital to the government. Morton, as Chancellor, presided at Council meetings if Henry were absent and he was ably seconded by Richard Fox, Bishop of Exeter, King's secretary and Lord Privy Seal. Other Councillors included Uncle Jasper, now Duke of Bedford, and the Stanleys (Lord Stanley became Earl of Derby : his wife preferred to sign herself simply 'Margaret R' – a title to which she had no shadow of a claim). Oxford became High Admiral of England, Constable of the Tower and keeper of the royal menagerie – with an allowance of 12d a day for himself and 6d a day for each lion or leopard in the Tower.

Of Henry's enemies, some had been killed at Bosworth, some were captured, and some fled to sanctuary. Richard himself and Norfolk were dead. Norfolk's son, Surrey, was imprisoned in the Tower with Northumberland – both were soon released and served Henry faithfully. Among those in sanctuary were Francis, viscount Lovell, and the two Stafford brothers – close followers of Richard. The critical figure was the earl of Lincoln, Richard's nephew and chosen heir. He was in his early twenties, an able soldier and an ambitious man. Like Surrey, he had fought against Henry at Bosworth, but unlike Surrey he was not imprisoned. He negotiated a pardon (probably from sanctuary somewhere), reappeared, and established himself at once as an important member of the Council.

It was a hard-working Council, and Henry drove himself equally hard. His meticulous accounts, checked and initialled by himself, show something of the care with which he supervised his affairs. He chose his subordinates well and the key to his success was the ever-increasing efficiency of his administration.

After the splendour of the coronation his first Parliament met (to confirm, not to create him King of England). They petitioned that he should marry the Princess Elizabeth – a marriage projected repeatedly during the previous years. Henry had, in fact, already asked Rome for the dispensation he needed to marry a fourth cousin twice removed. As soon as the Papal Legate gave a provisional dispensation the marriage took place. But her coronation had to wait.

When the spring came, Henry set out on a progress. Such a journey was undertaken partly to get into the country in the hot months when plague was at its worst, but it was chiefly designed to show the flag. The city of York had been especially devoted to Richard, going so far as to enter, when they heard of his death, the 'grete hevynesse of this Citie' in the minutes of the town council. So it was to York that Henry set out. As he went, minor rebellions broke out, headed by Lovell and the Staffords. They looked momentarily threatening, but Henry advanced resolutely, scraping together an armed force and offering the rebels a choice of pardon and reconciliation or excommunication and death. The risings sputtered out and Lovell fled to Lancashire where Sir Thomas Broughton sheltered him and where he was far beyond the King's reach. The Staffords took sanctuary at Abingdon near Oxford but the King and his Council decided that the church could not protect traitors and dragged them to the Tower, closely followed by the abbot, John Sante, coming to make the strongest possible representations to the Council. His protests were ineffectual: Humphrey Stafford was executed. His younger brother Thomas was pardoned, and walked quietly all the rest of his days.

Meanwhile, York had decided to make the best of the new situation, and its gates were opened with pageantry and a great show of welcome to the King and his retinue. Many of those who lined the streets must have fixed their eyes on the one man in that retinue who was well known to them already – the man who had been President of the Council of the North under Richard III – John de la Pole, earl of Lincoln.

From York the progress moved on to Worcester, Hereford, Gloucester and Brisol (where Henry showed a practical interest in the trade and prosperity of the merchants), before turning for home and London's civic welcome on the river. Then from London, in September, to Winchester. Henry was an efficient King and Elizabeth was proving herself efficient in her chief responsibility. She was to bear him seven children, three of them sons, but the first child was the critically important one. Henry arranged that the birth – the ceremonial of which was stage-managed by his mother – should take place in Winchester, the ancient capital of the country's legendary past. In the cathedral there hung the Round Table, which he painted with roses. And when Elizabeth gave him the son he needed, the baby was christened Arthur.

He now had a crown, a queen and an heir. His first year on the throne ended auspiciously.

4 The Dark Earl

The earl of Lincoln seemed to be reconciled to Henry and the new government, but Henry did not give him his trust. He remained on probation for eighteen months and more, his income and his honours less than they had been under Richard III. He must have watched other Council members acquiring lands and offices, and chafed in silence.

Much of the land around Oxford belonged or had belonged to Yorkists – Suffolk, Lincoln and the fugitive Lovell. Lovell had been one of the founders of the Guild of the Holy Cross at Abingdon (a charitable association of laymen who maintained the town bridge over the Thames) and members of the Guild followed him to Bosworth – for which they were pardoned by Henry. The town of Abingdon was largely run by the abbey, and the abbot, John Sante, had given the Staffords sanctuary and protested vigorously when they were taken and thrown into the Tower.

It is not surprising that it was in Oxford that William Symons (twenty-eight years old and a priest) dreamed that he was tutor to a King. When he woke, the likeliest candidate seemed to him to be Lambert Simnel, son of an organ-maker. He must have communicated the idea to Yorkists in the area, who took Simnel up and smuggled him away to Ireland. On 1 January 1487 John Sante and Christopher Swan (a yeoman who had been town-bailiff of Abingdon) put their heads together and decided to send a man called John Mayne abroad, Sante providing the money.

Mayne's departure had something to do with Simnel's. For in January Simnel appeared in Ireland, claiming to be Edward, earl of Warwick. The Council, Lincoln among them, decided to publicise the fact that the real Warwick was still in their hands. Somehow they had got hold of Symons, and a suitably public occasion was to hand. The leading churchmen of the country were gathering in London for the first Convocation of Henry's reign, which was to be held in St Paul's in February. Two special sessions could be stage-managed by Archbishop Morton.

So the leaders of the nobility and the mayor, aldermen and sheriffs of London were invited to St Paul's, first to hear Symons confess his part in the affair. Then, two days later, the real earl of Warwick was brought to meet the same group of people. Morton made him stand in front of him so that everyone could see him, and those who had known him as a little boy talked to him. It was two days before his twelfth birthday.

Among the members of the Council who saw and talked to him was his cousin, the earl of Lincoln. His eighteen months on probation had given him time to recover from the shock of Bosworth and from any gratitude he may have felt for Henry's clemency after the battle. Richard III had taught him to look forward to a throne and now he was working for a man who would be master in his house and who had his own son to follow him. Lincoln was a man of cold courage and calculation who saw in the Simnel conspiracy the great chance of his life.

Had the real Warwick escaped, there would have been little motive for Lincoln to rebel against Henry: he had no interest in knocking down one master to set up another. But an impostor could be joined and used until Henry was overthrown, after which he could be replaced by the strong man, Lincoln. So, having seen Warwick and established to his own satisfaction that Simnel was indeed an impostor, Lincoln slipped away to the Low Countries, to the court of his aunt, Margaret of Burgundy, the sister of Edward IV and Richard III. In her court were a number of exiled Yorkists, including Lovell, who had journeyed there after staying for a while with Sir Thomas Broughton in Lancashire.

Margaret provided Lincoln and Lovell with 2,000 German mercenaries, led by Martin Schwarz and paid for by herself, and they sailed for Ireland, landing on 5 May. Their arrival settled the minds of any remaining Irish doubters and Simnel was crowned as Edward VI at Christ Church in Dublin. He was lifted onto the shoulders of Darcy Platten, the tallest man in the town, so that people might see him, wearing a crown borrowed from a statue of the Virgin. But whoever got crowned in Dublin, Lincoln took immediate command of the soldiers and of tactics. Schwarz and Lovell, older men and more experienced soldiers, accepted him as leader. He cut short the rejoicings, packed Edward VI with his other luggage, and on 4 June landed at the Pile of Fouldry, Furness in Lancashire, where he was welcomed and joined by Sir Thomas Broughton.

Lincoln's flight turned Simnel from a cloud on Henry's horizon to a real and chilling threat. He tried to isolate him by offering a pardon to all rebels who surrendered, even including Sir Thomas Broughton, and he prepared for invasion. He seems to have expected one attack from Ireland and another, led by Lincoln himself, in East Anglia, where Lincoln was an important landowner and could expect support. So, pausing only to commit the marquis of Dorset (that early Tudor muggins) to the Tower, for no good reason except that he tended to be light-headed, Henry moved to Norwich, where he mixed the pious with the practical by visiting Walsingham and setting Oxford to raising levies.

The East Anglians seem to have dragged their feet, but Oxford got something of a force together, and Henry decided that, as the invasion was delayed, it would probably not come in that part of the country. He moved to Kenilworth, a central point where communications were good. Meanwhile Lincoln had his eyes on York, hoping that the city would rise on his side and provide him with a base and more men, so he set off to march across the Pennines. With him were Schwarz's experienced soldiers, some English exiles, Sir Thomas Broughton and his men, and a force of Irish, hardy and enthusiastic but ill-equipped and used to swift attacks rather than pitched battles. Altogether Lincoln's army numbered between eight and ten thousand men. Kings of England were remote, unimportant men to the northern English and few rose to join Lincoln as he marched: his hopes were on York.

In York, minds had changed. On 31 May, four days before Lincoln landed in Lancashire, a man called James Taite had been brought before the Mayor, aldermen and town councillors. Master Kalill, one of the King's chaplains, and three other men accused him of uttering treasonable words, saying that the earl of Lincoln would 'give the King's grace a breakfast'; that he would be helped by Sir Thomas Mallevery; and that during the King's visit to York in 1486 Lincoln had wanted to go 'over the walls' to join Robin of Redesdale (the Yorkshire Robin Hood).

Taite had denied the charge and told a different story. Early that spring — according to him — he had been to Retford, and on his way home on Lady Day — 25 March — at Doncaster he fell in with three merchants travelling north with their servants and seven horses. They were strangers to him, but he particularly noticed a white pony which they were leading. He talked to the servants, one of whom told him they were from London and showed him that the white pony's saddle was filled with gold and silver. Another servant, Saunders, asked Taite if there were any plague in York, and Taite reassured him. Then Taite told Saunders that he recognised the white pony because it had been stabled at his house during the King's visit to York the previous year. It belonged to the earl of Lincoln.

He asked after the earl and was told 'that he had departed from the King's grace. And I asked him whether to the sea or to the land, and he said, "I trow he need not go to the sea for he hath friends enough upon the land".' Saunders then asked where Sir Thomas Malleverey lived, as they were carrying letters to him. Taite asked if they were going to York and was told, 'Nay, I must to Hull. And if I come to York I will call upon you.'

At Wentbridge (on the great north road near Pontefract) he left the merchants and their servants asleep at an inn and rode north, meeting on the way another man whom he knew to be a follower of Lincoln's, who was hurrying to Wentbridge to meet the merchants. Taite went quietly on to York and soon afterwards Saunders came to see him and told him that his masters had an assignation with the prior of Tynmouth at the Blue Boar in Castlegate. A day or two later Taite uttered the words his companions took for treason. He maintained that he was doing his honest duty as a citizen, reporting treason to one of the King's chaplains. He added that during the King's visit to York two fellows who lived about Middleham and who ate and drank with Lincoln's household had said, 'Here is good gate for us to Robin of Redesdale over the walls.' 'And,' Taite finished indignantly, 'this I said and no word more, little or mickle.' Nobody asked him why he had waited several days before reporting the treason, but they did send for the ostler at the Blue Boar, who confirmed that the prior of Tynmouth had been lodging at the inn the previous

Monday and that the prior's servant had brought to him three merchants, travellers from the south.

The city council, having so recently committed themselves to Henry, were nervously anxious to prove their new loyalty. They immediately sent Taite, Kalill and the ostler under escort to the earl of Northumberland, and sent copies of the depositions to Richard Fox, the King's secretary. Their action was probably noted by Lincoln's friends within the city walls, who slipped out to meet the earl as he reached Tadcaster on his eastern march, and warned him that the gates would be closed to him. Lincoln's hope now lay in a swift blow while his forces were fresh and their spirits high. He turned south and marched through Castleford and along the old Ryknild Street (the Roman army's roads still governed the movements of any troops in a hurry). At Rotherham he forked half left and made along the high ground to Southwell, five miles west of Newark.

Henry's intelligence service was good. Five days after Lincoln reached Furness he heard the news and marched to Loughborough, where he received clear information that Lincoln was advancing down the eastern side of the Pennines. He moved to Nottingham, where he was joined by 6,000 men led by Lord Strange (Richard III's hostage, who had escaped at Bosworth). They captured some spies of Lincoln's and hanged them on an ash tree at the south end of the Trent bridge. Then Henry set out along the Fosse Way towards the fortified town of Newark.

Meanwhile Lincoln had decided to offer battle. Time was not on his side, and he must win quickly if he was to win at all. Realising that the King would be marching to Newark he decided to intercept him. Between Newark and Nottingham the river Trent, 150 yards wide, flowed through a marshy valley. In the summer it could be forded at Fiskerton and it was there that Lincoln crossed on Friday, 15 June. Next morning he drew his troops up in battle order, using the gentle hill to give himself the upper ground. His right flank extended to Burham furlong and was protected there by the steepish escarpment to the river, so it could not be turned.

There had been some trouble in Henry's army – they were not professionals like Schwarz's men, but civilians used to defending their homes but not to army discipline – and it took time on

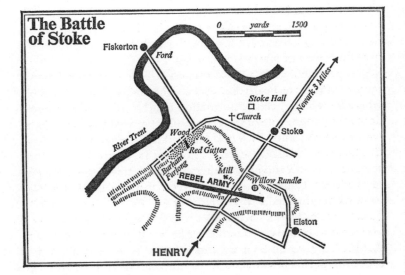

The Battle of Stoke

Fiskerton

Ford

0   yards   1500

River Trent

Newark 3 Miles

Stoke Hall
□

† Church

Wood

Stoke

Red Gutter

Burham Furlong

Mill

Willow Rundle

REBEL ARMY

Elston

HENRY

Saturday morning to get them out of bed and on the march, especially as the nearness of the enemy meant that they must march in battle order, divided into their three wards – the fore, main and rear. Oxford was in charge of the 6,000 men of the fore ward, the pick of the troops and the ones suffering least from the previous indiscipline. He had his troops formed up, each man in the place he must hold when he came to fight and therefore unable to straggle, before either of the other wards was ready. He moved off briskly and so became separated from the main ward under the King's command, which should have been immediately behind him.

His troops marched with their centre moving along the Fosse Way and the two wings stretching either side. Lincoln, in drawing up his troops, had done so with an eye to two tactical necessities: he must bar the road (which meant having his line of battle at ninety degrees to it) and he must cover his line of retreat to Fiskerton ford (which meant having it at forty-five degrees to the road). He compromised and drew his men up as they are shown in the map on page 26. This meant that when Oxford sighted them his left wing was closer to Lincoln's men than his right.

In any force of soldiers at this time, the right had the best soldiers and the left the weakest. Thus Oxford's weakest men were closest to Lincoln's strongest, and Lincoln's men had the advantage of the rising ground. Oxford must halt his men and alter the angle at which they were deployed, bringing his right wing forward. At any time this would be complicated and with a large force within sight of the enemy it was a very ticklish manoeuvre. Inevitably there was some confusion. Lincoln, confronted by an isolated and apparently confused fore ward, saw before him what seemed a magnificent chance to attack and put Oxford's troops to flight before the main ward could arrive. He had determined to fight a defensive battle, holding the advantage of the ground, but almost certainly he decided to attack at this point, and at first Oxford's troops were so shaken that some of them fled, spreading reports that all was lost.

As soon as he saw Lincoln, Oxford sent messengers back to the King, who hurried the best men from the main ward to reinforce him. His artillery was too slow-moving to come into action in time. The main body of Oxford's troops stood firm against Lincoln's men until the reinforcements arrived and turned the tide of battle. Schwarz and his professionals stood and were killed. The Irish, after fighting well in the initial attack on Oxford, were the first to break. Those who were fleeing headed for the ford, but on the path down the escarpment something held them up (perhaps a wagon wheel came off) and Oxford's men caught them up. The path is still called the Red Gutter.

More of Lincoln's men were killed after his army had broken than during the main battle. Four thousand of them died altogether, and three thousand of Henry's troops. Lincoln himself was killed with Schwarz and Sir Thomas Broughton. Lovell was seen making his horse swim the river, and never seen again – two years later Henry, presuming him dead, gave his widow a pension. Simnel was captured and Henry, with a proper sense of dramatic effect, made him a scullion. He worked in the royal kitchens for years, eventually winning promotion to falconer, and emerged momentarily into history again in 1493 when a group of Irish lords were at court and Henry brought Simnel in to serve them wine and drink their healths. 'My masters of Ireland,' he said as he watched, 'you will crown apes next.'

Meanwhile, having left the battle to the professional Oxford, Henry marched on to Lincoln, where many of the rebels were hanged, and then returned to London. We may count Stoke, not Bosworth, as the last battle of the Wars of the Roses.

In London he found that a group of men who had been in sanctuary at Westminster had heard the report of his defeat and had come out to plunder the houses of those who were known to be away at the battle. He wrote to the Pope, complaining of this danger inherent in the right to sanctuary and told him the story of one of these men, John Swit, who had said, 'And what signify censures of Church or Pontiff? Do you not perceive that interdicts of that sort are of no weight whatever, since you see with your own eyes that those very men who obtained such in their favour are routed and that the whole anathema has recoiled upon their own heads?' But, says Henry, 'On pronouncing these words he instantly fell dead upon the ground, and his face and body instantly became blacker than soot itself, and shortly afterwards the corpse emitted such a stench that no one soever could approach it.'

Having written his letter, Henry released Dorset from the Tower and turned his mind to planning the Queen's coronation in November. He took no action against James Taite. He fined abbot Sante two thousand marks (a mark was worth £$\frac{2}{3}$) letting him off when he had paid 802 of them, and leaving him to continue a varied career, which included entertaining the King at his abbey and becoming a member of the Council and an ambassador to France. In 1490 he was involved, with Christopher Swan, John Mayne and some others, in a project to free the earl of Warwick (now fifteen years old) from the Tower. They were all attainted for treason, their goods being forfeit but not their lives, and Sante was only pardoned, three years later, on the unpalatable condition that his monks sing a daily mass for King Henry and his family. After that he seems to have confined his considerable ability to completing the rebuilding of the abbey's gateway.

5 Interlude with Heresy

For all the disadvantages of his wandering, risky childhood, King Henry was a man of some education. He was a patron of poets as well as of musicians, and a considerable buyer of books and manuscripts – the first English king to build a palace containing a library. His Christianity was that of an intelligent, sophisticated man with a touch of Celtic mysticism about him, living in the last generation before the unity of Christendom was shattered by Luther and Calvin.

His piety was in tune with his generation. Throughout the country there was an outburst of church-building and he headed it, soaring to the intricate glory of high perpendicular. Such buildings framed a day-to-day piety which was a real force in his life. He had 'a singular devotion' to Our Lady and a respect for relics – a leg of St George was a prized possession. Throughout his reign there came acts of charity, endowments of hospitals and amnesties for prisoners. His will made detailed provision for the saying of ten thousand masses for his soul.

His generation could combine absolute belief in Catholic Christianity with a clear perception of the defects of a Church governed for most of his reign by the Borgia Pope, Alexander VI. The papacy was a spiritual and also a political power which could help to secure Henry's throne by excommunicating the opposition, ease his dyspepsia by licensing him to eat eggs and cheese in Lent, and help him dynastically by granting dispensations for royal marriages within the forbidden degrees of kin.

Some medieval ideals were recognised as mirages, to which lip-service only was due. Henry allowed the sale of indulgences to pay for a crusade, and installed a collecting box at court. The sale throughout the kingdom raised £49 and the box, when it was opened before the assembled dignitaries of the realm, was found to contain eleven guineas.

The wealth of the church was resented, especially that of the enclosed, self-regarding monks. A few of the weaker monasteries were investigated and closed during the reign. The spread of literacy among the laity pressed hard on the lower clergy, especially some parish priests who were ill-educated and impoverished. Richard Fox originally intended that his new college at Oxford should educate young monks; but he was persuaded that a new age was coming when laymen must be taught the new learning, and he altered the endowment. John Colet – scholar, friend of Erasmus, dean of St Paul's, and founder of a great school with a lay headmaster – was taking a fresh look at the bible as a source of true piety. He saw the Epistles of St Paul not as the mystic utterances of God, but as the letters of a man, accommodating what he said to the limitations of his readers, and he even took this approach into the Old Testament, describing the creation story in Genesis as a 'poetic figment' used by Moses to make God's intentions vivid to his primitive followers.

Morton closing weak religious houses; Fox endowing a college for laymen; Colet scraping scholastic barnacles off the Bible: these were all churchmen working within the church for a new age. There were others of a more revolutionary turn of mind. In England such men looked back to England's great heretic, John Wycliffe, who had died – in his bed – in 1380. He had seen, in the shattering waves of the Black Death, an expression of God's anger at the accumulated sins of men, and he called on society to return to the simplicity, the poverty and the teachings of Christ and his disciples, as they were revealed in the Bible. All things, he said, belonged to God. Man had only the use of material goods during his lifetime, and if he did not make good use of them he forfeited his right to them, cleric as much as layman. A man whose behaviour was not in harmony with that of the apostles was reprobate and beyond salvation, even if he were a priest. A reprobate pope (Wycliffe was living at a time when there were two competing popes) was an antichrist and in the hands of reprobate priests the sacraments lost authority, leaving man to turn to the Bible which – read with true humility – would give infallible guidance and salvation.

This insistence on the personal in religion – that nothing should interpose between the individual and his maker – led Wycliffe to condemn all ceremony and mystery, which tended to exalt the clergy above the laity. He condemned pilgrimages and images of the saints as idolatrous, and the blessing of things as magic. The confession of sins and the use of costly vestments and gold plate in church made the clergy arrogant and must be abolished. The mysterious change of bread and wine into the body and blood of Christ was magic and did not in fact take place, though at the consecration Christ became present with the bread and the wine. A priest's chief function was not to administer the sacraments, but to preach the word of God.

Wycliffe's cry for simplicity in many ways echoed those of successive reformers before him, and his poor priests – the lollards – resembled the early friars before success had made them fat and lazy. At first many lollards found a welcome. One or two great laymen (John of Gaunt, Henry VII's great-great-grandfather, among them) took it upon themselves to help the clergy back to a state of grace by seizing their property. But the lollards carried in their doctrine the slow fuse of civic as well as religious anarchy. If every man could find his own personal road to God in the pages of his own personal copy of the Bible, then every man might be equal, and that would do the gentry and nobility no good at all.

So lollards were persecuted and forced underground, to become a hidden, secret power in cottages and among working men in towns like London and Oxford. Their spirit can be traced in the contrast between friar and ploughman in *The Creed of Piers Plowman*. The friar is

> A great churl and a grim,
> Grown as a ton
> With a face so fat
> As a full bladder
> Blown bretful of breath,
> With a jowl lolling
> So great as a goose egg
> Grown all of grease,
> That all wagged his flesh
> As a quicksand.

While the ploughman works in torn clothes and patched mittens, helped by his wife, who is

Wrappen in a winnowing sheet
To ward her from weathers,
Barefoot on the bare ice
So that the blood follows.

And at the end of the strip of land is a crumb-bowl in which lies a baby wrapped in rags, with two toddlers crying beside it.

Lollardy, with its call for equality and the brotherhood of man, has an appeal to the twentieth century, though the wealthy might take a fifteenth-century view of abandoning their privileges and possessions. They might also ask how, without some sort of hierarchy, society is to be organised. There is a naïve idealism in thinking that any man, reading the Bible, will find God undistorted by his own prejudices, and Wycliffe's urge to simplicity led him to condemn all learning except Bible-reading – he threw out the civilised, cultural baby with the ceremonial bath-water.

Heresy was a spiritual infection, easily caught by one man from another. It was the duty of a careful bishop, as of a doctor, to isolate the sufferer and cure him if possible. But the good of the community must come first, and if the patient proved incurable the infection must be eradicated by fire. It was a logical and hygienic attitude of mind. Some of those convicted of heresy in the time of Henry VII were men of real sanctity, but many of them were simple people who combined vaguely Wycliffite notions with touches of witchcraft and perhaps some hysteric trick, such as levitation – today such people would be In Touch with the Occult or chatting to little men from flying saucers – and a conviction for heresy usually acted like a douche of cold water. Most of them abjured and confessed that they had been wrong. Abjuration and repentance returned the heretic to membership of the church, but the church was not to be made a fool of. A heretic could save himself from burning by abjuring the first time he was convicted, but a second conviction brought him to the stake, even if he abjured again, and a few men died that way.

The burning of one such man in 1498 is recorded in the contemporary *Chronicle of London*. 'In the beginning of May, the King being at Canterbury, was burnt an heretic, a priest, which by the King's exhortations before his death was converted from his erroneous opinions, and died a Christian man; whereof his grace got great honour.' The King himself, in his accounts, noted the gift to the man of an angel ($£\frac{1}{3}$) – a coin minted at the Tower in the gold which had been, to Wycliffe, a symbol of corruption.

6 The French Lad

The battle of Stoke in 1487 left the Yorkists leaderless and in complete disarray. It took them some time to reorganise. The first stirrings of a new attempt at the throne came in 1490 – the year when abbot Sante failed to engineer Warwick's escape from the Tower. In that year a man called John Taylor wrote from Rouen to a friend in England saying that the King of France would 'aid and support your master's son to his right', and a herald travelled from Ireland to Scotland and then to Burgundy. A new attempt was being discussed and a figurehead must be found for it.

Perkin Warbeck's parents were comfortable middle-class people. They had planned for him a life of trade and he first left his home at Tournai to go and learn Flemish – Flanders being a great centre of European trade. He wanted to see the world, and in due course took service with the wife of Sir Edward Frampton and travelled with her and her husband to Portugal in 1489.

As a converted Jew in England, Sir Edward had come into contact with Edward IV – the King was legal godfather to all Jews who received baptism. He had been a strong Yorkist, which was the reason for his exile. By 1489 he was anxious to come home and his services to Henry's envoys in Portugal during that year brought him a royal pardon. From him Warbeck would have learnt about King Edward's court, and from him Henry would later have learnt about Warbeck's background.

While he was in Portugal Warbeck entered the service of Pregent Meno, a Breton merchant. With Pregent Meno and John Taylor he travelled to Cork. According to the confession he later made to Henry, he was walking the streets as a model, wearing clothes made of the cloth his master wanted to sell, when he was hailed as the earl of Warwick, then as a bastard son of Richard III, and finally as Richard, duke of York (second son of Edward IV and the younger of the two little princes in the Tower). He allowed himself to be persuaded into saying he was Richard.

It is more likely that John Taylor was looking for a figurehead and chose Warbeck because of his appearance and his ability to carry things off with an air. He probably wore his clothes well and – although he had a cast in his left eye – looked a little like Edward IV. Edward had been well over six feet tall and very good looking in the style of the young Henry VIII, his grandson, and had been possessed of great charm and ingratiating manners (especially with women).

A 'court' formed itself about Warbeck, teaching him English among other things, but Ireland as a whole did not rise as it had done for Lambert Simnel. Better than Ireland seemed in view, however, for in 1492 Charles VIII invited Warbeck to France, where he was treated with great honour.

France was emerging as the strong, unified power in Europe, and her growing strength alarmed the other powers – the loose-knit Empire, the squabbling Italian states and Spain, whose new unity depended on the royal marriage of Ferdinand and Isabella. Henry felt himself threatened as well, especially in France's desire to appropriate the duchy of Brittany, with its good harbours directly to windward of England. He supported the duchess of Brittany in her struggle to keep her freedom, and when the struggle ended in capitulation and a marriage between the duchess and Charles VIII of France, he was outraged – English money and men had been wasted and he was now both threatened and looking foolish. He demanded compensation and began to prepare for war.

The idea of Henry VII winning back the lands and glories of Henry V appealed to the English, and they voted him money to pay the troops he was assembling at Portsmouth and for whom he was building three great breweries – beer was the English soldier's conquering spirit. In 1492 he formally invaded France. It cannot have been a very serious invasion, for military campaigns could only be carried on while the summer sun was keeping the roads dry, and Henry sailed for France in October, but it gave urgency to the negotiations which bishop Fox and Giles, first baron Daubeney, were carrying on with the French. Charles VIII was anxious to invade Italy as soon as possible, and did not haggle over terms: the Treaty of Étaples was signed on 3 November. Henry had been in the field for three weeks and in touch with the enemy (besieged in Boulogne) for nine days, with a loss of one knight.

Parliament had paid him to go to war and Charles VIII paid him to go home, with a steady income of 50,000 francs a year. For Henry it had been a profitable little war: for innumerable gentlemen who had gone with him in hopes of plunder, it was a confidence trick, and his popularity dropped steeply. This was not a King who would bring England glory.

For Perkin Warbeck it meant moving on. A clause in the Treaty of Étaples forbade either side to harbour the other's rebels, and he was asked to leave France. He went to Burgundy, where the dowager duchess Margaret welcomed him as she had welcomed Lincoln, and declared that she recognised him as her long-lost nephew. At her court were plenty of disappointed Yorkists ready to improve his English and his 'memory' of Edward IV's court. Margaret's chivalrous and erratic stepson-in-law Maximilian was equally ready to recognise him.

Having smoked Warbeck out of France, Henry now asked the Netherlands' Council of Regency, acting on behalf of the boy Archduke Philip, to expel him. They replied that the dowager duchess was a free agent within the dower lands. It is a measure of the seriousness which underlay Henry's studied unconcern about Warbeck that he imposed a trade embargo on the Netherlands to try to force them to do what he asked. It was an action which brought great hardship to both countries, and in London there were riots.

Warbeck was gathering support. His official life-story told how his elder brother (little Edward V) had been killed and he himself delivered 'to a gentleman who had received orders to destroy him, but who, taking pity on his innocence, had preserved his life, and made him swear on the sacraments not to disclose for a certain number of years his birth and lineage'. He had led a wandering and uncertain life for eight years with two guardians until one of them died and the other returned to England. At that time he was in Portugal: he went to Ireland and was recognised there. It was a tale which fitted the popular romances of the time and a number of countries were interested in England's being weak and divided. Warbeck was recognised as rightful King by France, Denmark,

Scotland, Saxony and many other states as well as by the young Philip of the Netherlands and his father, Maximilian. In November 1493 he joined other notables at the funeral of Maximilian's father, the emperor Frederick III, the Holy Roman Emperor, and afterwards Maximilian rode back to the Netherlands with him and established him at Antwerp in the house of the Merchant Adventurers – empty because of the trade embargo. He was given a guard of twenty archers with white roses in their hats and he displayed the arms of England on the house. In January 1495 he named Maximilian and Philip as his heirs if he died childless.

Henry had probably the best service of 'intelligencers' in Europe. These agents were a cross between the modern spy and newspaperman. Many respectable and godly merchants and travelling clerics wrote to him with the local news and gossip, receiving some small consideration and being subjected to ruthless cross-examination when they came home. Some were prominent men who liked their bread buttered on both sides – the earl of Bothwell and several other Scots lords were in Henry's pay. Others were agents who told of old conspiracies and infiltrated new ones. Pregent Meno, the Breton merchant, was in Henry's pay by 1496. Certainly a number of the Yorkists at the court of Margaret of Burgundy were red roses temporarily bleached.

Helped by his agents, Henry watched conspiracy at home and abroad, hoping that the conspirators would give up the dangerous game as they lost faith in Warbeck. One who does seem to have done so was Sir Robert Clifford. He had been with the army in France and had acted as interpreter during the peace negotiations. Later he joined Warbeck in the Netherlands, declaring that he recognised him. He was a considerable name for Warbeck to have on his side. He may have changed his mind as he came to know Warbeck; he may have been bought by Henry; or he may have been Henry's agent throughout. However it was, in December 1494 he and his servant were pardoned and returned to England. A wave of arrests followed. Three leading clerics (one of them the Dean of St Paul's) were sent to prison and some prominent laymen were executed.

Most important of all was Sir William Stanley, part-victor at

Bosworth, brother to Margaret Beaufort's husband and Lord Chamberlain of the royal household. Henry had a reputation for being loath to hear or believe ill of anyone, and he may have been watching Sir William for a long time before he moved. Sir William, for all that he was one of the richest and most powerful men in the kingdom, may have felt that the King was ungrateful for his help at Bosworth, and have resented the fact that no earldom had come his way.

Henry spent Christmas 1494 at Greenwich, and then moved at once to the Tower where Sir Robert Clifford, newly home and newly pardoned, was interrogated. Sir William Stanley was summoned to court, finding when he arrived that the Tower was a prison as well as a palace, and from the end of January to the middle of February the conspirators were tried, sentenced and either reprieved or executed, ending with the most important prisoner, Sir William. Those involved included members of the clergy, of the King's own household, and of the vital and vulnerable garrison of Calais. The seven clergymen were reprieved and later pardoned. Three of the gentry and Sir William were beheaded, and three were imprisoned. Three commoners were hanged, drawn and quartered and two reprieved on the scaffold because of their youth. One of those reprieved was Thomas Astwood, steward of Marton Abbey, whose path was to cross Warbeck's again years later.

The execution of Sir William Stanley was bound to have an effect on the royal family. It did not shake his brother's loyalty or break the close affection existing between Margaret Beaufort and her son, but they withdrew from court a little, spending more time on their scattered country estates – at Torrington in Devon, at Latham and Knowsley in Lancashire, in the fen country around Cambridge and most frequently at Colly Weston in Northamptonshire, where the King and Queen visited them during their summer progress. Margaret Beaufort turned increasingly to her charitable work and patronage – she was a patron to the early printers, Caxton and Wynkyn de Worde, and herself translated part of The Imitation of Christ into English for publication, and she helped to found St John's College and Christ's College at Cambridge.

While Henry dealt with conspiracy at home, his trade embargo was making the Netherlands anxious to be decently rid of Warbeck. Maximilian gave him fourteen ships, and he sailed away to seize the crown, appearing off Deal on 3 July 1495. He proved himself to be no good Plantagenet by not landing himself, but two or three hundred of his followers did. The local people, led by the Mayor of Sandwich, rounded them up and they were sent by the cartload to London. During the next two months they were tried and sentenced. Henry's usual clemency deserted him and they were taken to Wapping, to Tyburn and to the coast and hanged as a warning to other invaders – their bodies left swinging in the sea-breezes along the shores of Kent, Essex, Suffolk and Norfolk.

Meanwhile Warbeck had sailed on to Ireland and then – Ireland proving hostile – to Scotland where he was welcomed by James IV and given Lady Catherine Gordon, a distant cousin of the King's, as a wife. James also gave him a pension of £112 a month, but there is no record of its having been regularly paid to him.

Meanwhile political events had been moving in Henry's favour. Charles VIII had invaded Italy with meteoric success and frightened the European powers out of their perennial game of double-crossing each other. Spain, Maximilian, the Papacy, Venice and Milan formed the Holy League against France, and Henry found everyone wooing him as a potential ally. Both Spain and France offered to seize Warbeck's parents and send them to London.

In January 1496 all the ambassadors to Maximilian met to persuade him to renounce Warbeck. He – in his knight-errantry – said he 'considered it his duty not to abandon the duke' and offered to negotiate a ten-years' peace between Henry and Warbeck. The ambassadors replied heatedly that such a proposal would only irritate Henry. Maximilian gave way. Henry had 'arrived' as an established King and a European power. Trade between England and the Netherlands began again.

The Scottish court cannot have been altogether comfortable for Warbeck. The Sieur de Concressault, who had been captain of his bodyguard at the French court, was there – with 100,000 crowns in his pocket – trying to buy Warbeck from James as a present for Henry. A Spanish envoy was there, counterbidding with a Spanish princess in marriage for James (all the Spanish princesses were pledged, but Ferdinand was not one to let detail stand in his way). Roderick Lalaing from Flanders was there – an old associate of Warbeck's, now giving him the cold shoulder.

But James was planning the invasion which was to sweep Warbeck onto his throne. In gratitude before the event Warbeck gave James the town of Berwick which his father had taken from James's father. The invasion in September turned out to be a large-scale border raid. It was Warbeck's first sight of real war and he protested against the killing of his 'subjects'. His squeamishness did him no good in James's eyes – he pointed out that not a single Englishman had come forward to join them and told Warbeck that he concerned himself overmuch about a land which showed very little interest in him. Side by side, Warbeck saddened and James elated by the expedition, they rode back to Scotland. And from the border counties messengers hurried south to tell Henry that his kingdom had been invaded.

7 A Fly in the Ointment

James Taite, travelling in Yorkshire as Lincoln was preparing to invade England, had met merchants who were also agents spreading conspiracy through the country. James Taylor and Pregent Meno were merchants who helped to set Perkin Warbeck on his quest for a crown, and similar merchants spread a network of conspiracy through Europe in the years of his quest. They were – apart from official diplomatic commissions – the only people with legitimate reasons for travelling and for sending letters and money abroad. They played a game which was countered by Henry's 'intelligencers', many of whom were merchants themselves.

They used simple code in their letters. For instance, William de Noyon, a friar and a follower of Warbeck, wrote several letters on his behalf to Sir John Kendal, grand prior of the Order of St John of Jerusalem, who was eagerly following events from England. When Perkin was first in Flanders, de Noyon wrote to Sir John saying, 'The merchant of Roubaix could not sell his merchandise in Flanders for the price he wanted, so he has gone to the court of the King of the Romans to see if he can do better there' – meaning that Warbeck could not find in Flanders all the help he needed to invade England and had gone to seek aid from Maximilian.

Warbeck needed this correspondence to ensure that his friends in England were ready to come to his help when he invaded. When his men attacked Deal, Sir John Kendal was at a house of his order at Milbourne in Bedfordshire, knowing that the attack was to come and holding his men ready to fight on either side, their jackets being made reversible, ready to mount the red rose on one side or the white rose on the other. Sir John was an old enemy of Henry's. Before pinning his hopes on Warbeck, he had spent some time and money on an attempt to eliminate the King scientifically. His allies in this undertaking had been his nephew, Sir John Tong, a knight of the Order of St John of Jerusalem; William Hussey, the archdeacon of London and chancellor to the bishop; the archdeacon's nephew, John Hussey; Sir John's secretary, William Wotton; and several servants, one of whom was a Frenchman called Bernard de Vignolles.

Sir John Kendal, Sir John Tong and archdeacon Hussey were in Rome in 1492. They were anxious to bring about the deaths of Henry VII, his children, his mother and leading members of his Council. With this in mind they approached a Spanish astrologer called Radigo – Hussey went to lodge with him – but Radigo said he could not help them. They found another Spanish astrologer, Master John, who said he could do what they wanted. They asked for proof of his powers and he said that he had scruples about killing a Christian just to prove a point, but that the Grand Turk's brother was being held hostage at the Vatican just then and he would cause the death of one of his servants. He did so, and they agreed to pay him his price for similarly disposing of the English government.

They returned to England, leaving one of their continental contacts, a Sardinian called Stephen Marenecho, to keep an eye on their affairs. They sent Marenecho money through the bank to pay Master John, who refused to act because he said they had not sent enough – he later told Bernard de Vignolles that this first payment was only a retainer. So the matter was dropped, and for two years nothing was done. Then the conspirators heard that Radigo had been talking about their approach to him, and they decided to send Bernard de Vignolles to Rome with a double mission: to eliminate Radigo and to find Master John and tell him that he would receive the rest of his fee once he had produced results. They were also nervous because Master John had talked of coming to England to do the job personally, and they were afraid he would be recognised and arrested.

Whether Bernard de Vignolles accomplished the first part of his mission we cannot tell – the whole story comes from his own sworn deposition, and he was reticent on that point. He did find Master John, who was making elaborate plans for travelling to England by sea, disguised as a friar, having first replaced two missing teeth with false ones, made of ivory and stained to match his own. Bernard dissuaded him, saying he couldn't raise the fare, and asking that he kill the King by remote control.

Accordingly, Master John gave Bernard a little wooden box with ointment in it. It was to be given to Sir John Kendal, who was to smear the ointment on the frame of a doorway through which the King would pass. As soon as he had done so, those who had the greatest love for him would fall on him and kill him.

Astrologers and alchemists inspired the respect and credulity which we today reserve for anyone who talks a scientific language which is above our heads, or produces scientific miracles beyond our comprehension; and it was an age when many deaths came suddenly and inexplicably. Christians dying in hot weather would cry 'poison' and point to the healthy Jews living near them, rather than thinking to blame the stale pork which they ate and the Jews did not. Death being so capricious and poison so often suspected – especially if the death was of a politically important person and suited someone else's turn – it is no wonder that Master John and his miraculous ointment were given credence.

Bernard took the box back to his lodgings, where curiosity overcame him and he opened it. The smell was so appalling that he immediately closed it again and threw it down the privy. Next day he set off to travel overland to England. His thought-processes must have been slow, for it was not until he reached Orleans that it occurred to him that Master John might have written to Sir John Kendal, mentioning the ointment. When he did think of it he went to an apothecary and bought a similar box and some mercury. He took them back to his lodgings and mixed the mercury with earth, soot and water, making a paste which looked like the original, even if he could not recapture the original, vital stench. Then he travelled on to England and showed the box to Sir John Kendal. He probably foresaw possible trouble if his ointment were used and complaints made that it did not work. So he warned Sir John that the astrologer had told him it was very dangerous for anyone with evil plans to touch it, and also that there would be great danger if it remained for twenty-two hours in the same house with such a person. Sir John immediately told him to take the box a long way off and throw it away where it would not be found. Bernard obeyed.

During the next six months Bernard was too ill to travel, but as soon as he recovered he asked leave to visit his parents in France.

The conspirators were glad to have him overseas as they were by now in a thoroughly edgy state – worried lest he be arrested and forced to confess what had been going on. Bernard himself wanted to turn King's evidence but was too afraid of his master to go to the authorities in England. So he wrote to his brother in Dieppe, telling him to expect him, and once he was in France made his way to Rouen where, on 14 March 1496, he revealed the whole nefarious plot to one of the King's agents. His deposition was made in French – his native language – and endorsed, in the handwriting of Henry VII, 'La confession de Bernart de Vignolles'. Filed with the deposition are a few letters from the conspirators which were intercepted. One at least of these seems to be an answer to a letter from Bernard written after he had made his deposition, so probably he was asked to become a double agent for the time being.

Henry must have felt, as he so often did, that there was not enough evidence to justify moving against the conspirators, especially as it would have meant another big and showy trial only a year after the Stanley executions – sending the archdeacon of St Paul's to join the dean! As it was, the archdeacon remained archdeacon. Sir John Kendal kept his place and his liberty. It perhaps appealed to Henry's ironic sense of humour to make him – three years later – one of the Commissioners who presided at the trial of his 'merchant of Roubaix'.

8 The New Found Land

Europe has always imported its spices from the far east. The long journey made them expensive but men who had to salt down most of their cattle in the autumn and eat them in progressive stages of decay through the winter had a lively interest in anything which could mask the natural taste of high cow. Spices were essential: was there no easier way of getting them than by the caravan routes through heathen lands?

Long before the birth of Christ, Aristotle watched the shape of the earth's shadow crossing the moon in an eclipse, noticed the difference in the stars as seen from different countries, and concluded that the earth was round and that 'there is but a narrow sea between the western points of Spain and the eastern border of India'. It was an idea which lay dormant through the middle ages. Interest in the Indies was whetted by Marco Polo's account of his travels in the lands of the Great Khan and of the wealth he saw, not only in spice and silk but also in jewels and precious metals.

During the tenth century the Vikings, reaching out to the west, had discovered and colonised successively Iceland, Greenland and North America. The American colony was too distant to be successful in face of the hostility of the natives, but for many years Greenland and Iceland went west to find fish and timber. Then, in the fifteenth century, a change of climate brought ice and Eskimoes south to threaten the Greenland settlement. The last ship from Greenland to Iceland probably sailed in 1410 and the colony, unable to feed itself properly, dwindled slowly and died out. The last Greenlander probably died at about the time when Columbus sailed.

History is not only a matter of the written word. The men of Iceland knew of the great land to the west and their knowledge was not the prerogative of scholars: it belonged to seamen, handing it down through the generations, watching the currents of the Atlantic and noticing that, at certain seasons, driftwood floated in from the west. Modern navigational instruments and radio have made us forget and even despise the ancient skills, but still, in our own century, fishermen, cut off from the stars by fog or clouds, have conned their ships home by such currents and such flotsam.

Tales of the Norse discoveries may have been known to Columbus. It is much more than likely that they were known to the sailors of Bristol, for the Icelanders – against the orders of their government in Norway – traded with Bristol. Mixed with the truth was legend – tales of mysterious islands, monstrous beasts and mythical riches – but there was enough reality in the tradition to persuade Bristol to send men to look for 'the island of Brasylle'. An expedition sailed in 1480, wandered for nine months and returned without finding anything, and in 1498 the Spanish ambassador was writing home to say that 'the people of Bristol have, for the past seven years, sent out every year two, three or four light ships, in search of the island of Brasil'. The successful expeditions were those led by John Cabot.

Cabot was probably born in Genoa, one of the two great trading cities of Italy, and in 1476 he became a naturalised citizen of the other – Venice. His wife was a Venetian and for a dozen or so years after his naturalisation he worked in the spice trade, travelling to the near east and into Arabia. During this time his three sons – Ludovico, Sebastian and Sancio – were born, and he began to think that he might find a way to the spices of the east by way of the western ocean. Such an enterprise was more likely to be supported by westward-looking countries than by those locked in the Mediterranean. Cabot tried to interest Portugal and Spain in helping him, and failed. In 1490, two years before Columbus sailed, he came to England with his family.

He must have had a struggle during the next six years. Sailing in the Atlantic is a very different matter from sailing in the Mediterranean, and he had to establish his credibility as a captain and as a navigator. In the meantime Columbus had both strengthened and weakened his case. He had proved the existence of land to the west, by discovering Cuba and claiming that it was the mainland of Asia. This discovery had led, in 1493, to an agreement between Spain and Portugal, embodied in and given authority by a bull issued by the Pope. This bull (slightly amended in 1494) drew a line down the globe, from north to south, three hundred and seventy leagues west of the Cape Verde Isles. Everything to be discovered west of the line was to be Spanish, and east of the line Portuguese. The line gave modern Brazil to Portugal, and the rest of the Americas to the Spanish – who still thought they had their hands on the Indies. Thus the new world was known to be accessible, but it was divided equably between Spain and Portugal. England and other countries were excluded.

Henry VII was a good son of the church, but he recognised the papal bull of 1493 as a political act, not a spiritual one. He would respect the right of Spain or Portugal to land which they had actually discovered, but claimed for himself the right to annex discoveries made under the English flag. So, on 5 March 1496, Henry VII issued from his palace at Westminster letters patent empowering John Cabot, his three sons, their heirs and their deputies, to sail under the English flag with five ships to all coasts of the eastern, western and northern seas, and to discover, annex, conquer and occupy in the King's name any lands hitherto unknown to Christians. They were to be exempt from customs on goods brought back by them, but were to pay the King one fifth of their profits, and no other subjects of the King were to resort to the lands they discovered without their permission. Had they under this licence discovered a land with, say, plenty of pepper to export to England, they would have become enormously rich almost overnight on their return.

Clearly Cabot had concluded that Columbus had not, in fact, discovered the mainland of Asia, or even the rich islands of Cipangu (Japan). Henry's grant excluded him from following the southern route to the west – Columbus's route. He intended to sail almost due west from Bristol, to discover the northern part of Asia. Once that had been found, further expeditions could coast south until they reached the rich cities of the Great Khan which Marco Polo had described. Cabot had no capital himself, but he had Bristol merchants behind him and on 2 May 1497 he sailed in the *Matthew* with a crew which included at least two of those merchants. On 24 June they sighted either Newfoundland or Nova Scotia and sailed south-west along the coast far enough to satisfy themselves that this was a continent and no outlying island that they had discovered. They saw signs of human habitation, and the absence of cities and wealth was easily explained: they were much farther north than the part of the continent visited by Marco Polo.

They turned for home, reaching Bristol, with a following wind, on 6 August. People in Bristol and London flocked to see 'the great admiral' on his way to a private audience with the King. 'To him that found the new isle,' wrote Henry's accountant, '£10,' and the gift was followed by a pension of £20 a year. Richly dressed, he gave a lecture at court on his findings, showing maps and globes and describing his hopes of spices and his observation of rich fishing-grounds. From that moment England became independent of the Icelandic fishermen and the cod of the Newfoundland fishery began to bring their own, unromantic riches to the ports of south-west England.

In May 1498 Cabot sailed again, this time with five ships richly laden with goods to be traded for the silks and spices of the Great Khan's subjects. They were to make a landfall as before, and then coast south-westwards to Cathay and Cipangu. There seems to have been some thought of founding a colony in the northern latitudes already discovered, perhaps as a base for traders and fishermen, and the King promised to supply convicts for the labouring involved, but the plan did not mature.

The expedition met heavy weather and one ship put back into an Irish harbour. There is no further direct evidence that anyone from the remaining four ships came home to tell of their discoveries. Yet in 1500 a Spanish map was published which shows a great stretch of coastline dotted with English flags, with such inscriptions as 'mare desubierto por inglese'. In 1501 a Portuguese ship following the course taken by Cabot found a European sword and ear-rings in the hands of a native in the neighbourhood of Newfoundland (Cabot had sighted no people on his first expedition, so someone must have got there the second time). And – also in 1501 – the Spanish sovereigns sent an expedition to sail north from established Spanish discoveries specifically 'setting up marks with the arms of their Majesties, so that you may stop the exploration of the English in that direction'.

It seems likely that some at least of the ships in Cabot's expedition carried out his intention, sailing south-west far enough to realise that this land was not Cathay, and that someone returned to tell the tale. People who carry disappointment home do not become celebrated at court and noticed by the chroniclers, which may be why the evidence for the return is so tenuous. The pension to John Cabot ended towards the end of 1499: perhaps because he was then presumed to be dead, and perhaps because someone had come home who knew he was lost.

The Portuguese, sailing from the Azores, turned north in 1499 and rediscovered Greenland. It was found by a 'llabrador' or minor member of the gentry, and for a time came to be known as Terra de Labrador, until the old Norse name re-established itself and the name Labrador moved west. More Portuguese had recognised that America was not Cathay and were looking for a north-west passage round the top of it. The only thing they established was a tradition of ships which set out and did not return.

In March 1501 Henry VII gave letters patent to three such Portuguese and to three Bristol merchants: Thomas Asshehurst, Richard Warde and John Thomas. They were to annex heathen lands between those discovered by John Cabot and those found by the Greenland expeditions – this again looks like the start of a search for the north-west passage. They sailed in 1501 and again in 1502 and each time won an entry in the King's accounts – 'to men of Bristol that found the Isle' and 'to the merchants of Bristol that have been in the New Found Land'. The first time it was £5 only, but the second time it was £20 and in addition two of the Portuguese got a pension of £10 a year 'in consideration of the true service they have done unto us to our singular pleasure as captains into the New Found Land'. Henry must have felt that they had found something worthwhile, and perhaps was pleased with the three savages they brought home as presents to him and whom he eventually managed to convert to the ultimate grace of looking like Englishmen.

Further voyages were made by the Company Adventurers into the New Found Lands. Their leaders changed – Richard Warde and John Thomas dropped out and Hugh Elyot (who may have been on the Matthew for John Cabot's first voyage) joined them. By 1506 they were involved in the national English sport of suing each other. A change came into the terms of their royal patent, too.

In December 1502 Henry empowered them to 'recover' – not just to 'discover' – heathen lands in any part of the world. He had moved from acknowledging Spanish and Portuguese claims to any lands they found to acknowledging them only where the land was actually occupied. It was a precedent followed by his grand-daughter Elizabeth in the teeth of Spanish opposition. He was clearly contemplating colonisation, for he elaborated on how such lands were to be governed, but no record survives to tell us whether or not any colony was in fact attempted.

Of John Cabot's three sons only the second, Sebastian, has any place in history – the others probably died young. Sebastian, who would have been in his early teens when his father sailed on his voyage of 1497, lived and worked in Bristol and in the spring of 1509 set out with two ships to find a North West Passage. When he came back he was sure he had found it – almost certainly he had reached Hudson's Bay – but his men had forced him to turn back because they were frightened of the ice-floes and the cold of the approaching winter. Henry VII had died on 22 April, soon after Sebastian sailed, and his son, who had married a Spanish princess, was more interested in his right to the throne of France than in the Americas. So Sebastian left England and from 1512–48 he worked in the service of Spain, coming back to England for the last ten years of his life to be consulted by a new generation of sailors, and to leave at his death in 1557 a mass of charts and papers which excited the Elizabethans and which have since disappeared.

9 The Cornish Rising

The border raid which James IV had carried out in September 1496 had alarmed the English government. It was on a larger scale than usual, led by James IV himself, and undertaken in the name of a Pretender to the English throne: it might well preface a full-scale invasion. Parliament was sufficiently worried to agree to the government's request for heavy taxes, to pay for an army to fight the Scots. The taxes were to be collected in May and November 1497, so in the spring the tax-collectors set out.

Those who went to Cornwall were going into a wild, remote province where the population spoke Cornish in preference to English, communicated with Brittany more easily than with England, and had hardly heard of Scotland. They made a living farming, mining and fishing. The miners were mostly self-employed men, living on the hope of a lucky strike and suffering as inflation and the increased cost of mining more and more deeply added to money problems created by the dealers who bought and often failed to pay for their tin. The fishermen had a lively export trade, selling smoked fish to Italy and Spain, and salt fish to France. They traditionally supplemented this income with a little piracy on the side but once Henry VII was firmly in the saddle he discouraged this, at the cost of his popularity in the province. He was not able to enforce his peace quickly or easily – the Cornish were in the habit of being lawless and they continued to be so. Most of the offences were the traditional ones – house-breaking, cattle-lifting, theft of tin and assault. One or two men almost made a profession of violence, as did Roger Whalley, a servant of Sir Richard Nanfan, who was one of Henry's most trusted diplomats. At one time Whalley was charged with twenty-six offences, including cattle-lifting, killing sheep and refusing to pay his tithes. He seems to have disliked his neighbour, John Trenowth, and had assaulted him, beaten his wife and shot through his windows.

The government exempted the poor from taxation, but not all

The Tower of London, seen from the river.
An early eighteenth-century engraving showing
clearly the opening where boats could be rowed up to
Traitor's Gate

Water Lane in the Tower.
On the right is St Thomas's Tower, built over Traitor's Gate.
The great gateway on the left leads through the Bloody Tower,
and the circular building beyond it is the Wakefield Tower

Anno 1505 20 october nwago henrick vii tranertes rege illustrissim̄
ordinata p herman̄ znick sō regie · · · · · · · · · · · · ·

Henry VII. A portrait painted in 1505 by Michael Sitium

Henry VII. Head of the effigy carried at his funeral:
the face is modelled from a death-mask

ELIZABETHA · VXOR
HENRICI · VII ·

Elizabeth of York, Henry VII's Queen

Margaret Beaufort, Countess of Richmond and Derby
mother of Henry VII

Catherine of Aragon,
painted by Miguel Sittoz
at about the time of her wedding
to prince Arthur

Perkin Warbeck

Henry VII's chapel. at Westminster Abbey —
the Tudor rose, the Beaufort shield and the French lily
mingle with intricate tracery to the greater glory of God
and His servant, the King

Henry checks the accounts. The first entry here reads:

Master Bray

27 August   Item. Received of Master ~~By~~ Bray by
              thands of William Cope of the Reveneuz   £108
              of thisle of Wight due at Ester last passed

Henry's sign-manual is at the right of each item —
at the second item on this page, on 28 August, 1492,
he changed his way of writing it

the tax-collectors were so gentle. In Cornwall there was one in particular who was especially severe. He was Sir John Oby, provost of Glasney College by Penryn. Within his area was the parish of St Keverne (down by the Lizard) where the village blacksmith was a man of great strength, courage and magnetism, called Michael Joseph.

The unrest seems to have started in his parish, and he led the rising. He was joined by a few of the minor gentry, some yeomen and a great many commoners, and they marched to Bodmin, where they were joined by Thomas Flamank, a lawyer and the son of one of the four commissioners who were in Cornwall assessing what taxes should be paid – a son rising against his father. He gave the rising its reasoning and managed to give it a peaceful, legal gloss. Scotland, he said, was too remote for Cornwall to be concerned in Scots wars, and the great lords of the north enjoyed their privileges because they – and they alone – were responsible for keeping the Scots in Scotland. The war was made 'to poll and pill the people' and the Cornishmen on the march were seeking, of pure love and loyalty, to free the King from his evil councillors – Morton and Bray – who had misguided him into oppressing his subjects. Francis Bacon, himself a lawyer, looked back over more than a century to the rising and remarked that Flamank talked 'as if he could tell how to make a rebellion, and never break the peace'.

The rebels marched peacefully through Taunton to Wells, where they were joined by James Touchet, Lord Audley, with whom they had already been in contact. His family had fought for Henry VI and Audley himself had been on two of Henry VII's continental excursions, in 1489 to help the Bretons against the French and in 1492 to besiege Boulogne. He was probably out of pocket and therefore out of temper on both occasions, and felt the King was ungrateful and unjust to him. His accession to their cause was a triumph to the rebels, though Michael Joseph and Flamank seem to have continued as leaders, with Audley as a figurehead.

So far the people had risen to help them – even some Cornish members of the Wells cathedral chapter. Now they marched east, half expecting Kent, with its tradition of Wat Tyler and

Jack Cade, to rise to meet them. In fact Kent did no such thing.

The government was taken completely by surprise, which is understandable in an age when governments were used to being threatened by overmighty lords, not by working men. But in the cause of the rising lay its defeat. It was a protest against taxes raised to pay an army. The army recruited to fight the Scots was available to put down the Cornish. Henry and his court were at Richmond when news of the true gravity of the situation arrived. He had to hand an army of 8,000 men under Lord Daubeney. He immediately sent Surrey north to Durham to hold the border and dispatched Daubeney to reconnoitre and assess the strength and intentions of the Cornish.

Surrey found James IV in no very serious mood. He was again raiding England, besieging bishop Fox in Norham castle – Fox in typically capable manner organised the defences and then improved the plumbing so that the water-supply should be better in time for any future siege – and he was galloping about the country enjoying the summer weather and a spell of hunting humans instead of animals. He challenged Surrey to single combat but it was impossible to induce him to fight a pitched battle, and he returned once again over the border leaving the diplomats to pick up the pieces.

Back in England the first essential was to keep the Cornish south of the Thames. As far back as 1066 London had proved impregnable from the south and William the Conqueror had been forced to cross the river at Wallingford and approach along the north bank. Now Henry himself moved from Richmond to hold Henley bridge sending the Queen and little Henry, duke of York, to the Tower for safe-keeping. He sent a messenger to Ewelme, near Oxford, to summon Edmund de la Pole to come and hold Staines bridge. Edmund de la Pole was the younger brother of the earl of Lincoln who had died at Stoke. He had been brought up under the King's eye and in his favour and was an erratic, headstrong young man-about-court, a good man in a tournament and – at this time – with no apparent wish to follow his older brother's star.

When the King's messenger arrived to summon him to hold

Staines bridge against the Cornish it was early morning, and the messenger hurried straight into Suffolk's bedroom, where he was still asleep. Also in the bed was young Lord Bergavenny (beds were few and large and the house was crowded). Hearing the door open and footsteps approaching the bed curtains, Bergavenny hid under the bedclothes while Suffolk sat up to hear the King's commands. When the messenger had gone Bergavenny emerged and Suffolk asked him, 'Why shrinkest thou and hidest thyself so? Art afeared?'

'Nay,' answered Bergavenny, and added, 'If a man will do aught, what will you do? Now is the time' – cryptic words which suggested that they might debate between courses of action – in other words that they might perhaps join the rebels.

'Ah,' cried Suffolk, 'wilt thou so?' and he immediately leapt out of bed, dressed, and rode away with his troops and Bergavenny's shoes, thus momentarily immobilising him. Years later, in 1506, Bergavenny's words were remembered and cost him some time in the Tower.

In the meantime, however, Suffolk – stuffing Bergavenny's shoes in his saddlebag – rode off to hold Staines bridge, and the Cornish were shepherded along, south of the river. They were fended off from Kent and the night of Thursday, 15 June found them camping on Banstead Down, south of London. Lord Daubeney was at St George's Fields, protecting London, and that night some of the rebels approached him, offering to surrender Audley and Michael Joseph in return for a general pardon. They did not offer Flamank, so perhaps he was behind the move – feeling their situation to be hopeless and trying to end it with little bloodshed. The offer was refused.

Next day the rebels moved to Blackheath and the King joined his troops. The Mayor lined the streets from London Bridge to Gracechurch Street with aldermen and all the crafts of the city. All turned out armed for battle so that the King could see them as he passed by. He spent the night at Lambeth in the tradition of Henry V before Agincourt, 'abrewing and comforting his people' – except that his 25,000 men were facing not a larger French army but a mob of farmers, fishermen and miners who were 'in great agony and variance' according to the chronicler, debating whether to yield to the King's mercy or to fight it out. Michael Joseph was resolute for fighting, and he carried his men with him.

At Deptford Strand the Ravensbourne flows into the Thames. As the short summer night ended, Henry and Daubeney could see that the Cornish had placed archers to hold the bridge across it and that their main force was well back from the bridge on the rising ground – too far away to come to the archers' rescue if they gave way. At first light Henry sent a force under Oxford, Essex and Suffolk – who had left Staines bridge once the Cornish were past it and the danger there over – to cut off the rebels' retreat to the south. He held himself in reserve and sent Daubeney to attack the bridge at Deptford Strand.

Sir Humphrey Stanley and his spearmen launched their attack at six o'clock. The bridge was well-defended – the strength of the Cornish bowmen amazed the Londoners – but the archers had no support and Daubeney was soon able to cross the bridge and attack the main force of the rebels, leading the charge himself so vigorously that for a time he was cut off and taken prisoner. But resistance was brief and the army soon held the field. Audley and Flamank were taken prisoner at once. Michael Joseph managed to get away and tried to reach sanctuary at the Observant Friars' at Greenwich, but he was taken before he could get there.

Henry followed his victorious army on to the field, knighted a number of his men, and by two o'clock was riding across London Bridge, the afternoon sun glinting on his armour, to be welcomed by the Mayor and his 'brethren in scarlet'. He thanked them for the preparations they had made and for provisioning the army and then, 'with his own sword which was girt about him', knighted the Mayor, one of the Sheriffs and the Recorder before going on to St Paul's to give thanks and make an offering. The City had been spectacularly saved within sight of its citizens: a most satisfactory result.

While Henry was in the cathedral Michael Joseph was brought through the streets to join Audley and Flamank in the Tower. He was riding behind a yeoman of the guard, wearing a jacket of white and green (the King's colours) 'and held as good countenance and spake as boldly to the people as he had been at his liberty'. After the service the King went to the Tower to spend

Sunday with his family and then, on Monday, to interrogate the three leaders of the rising. They were tried and condemned a week later, the King's mercy allowing that Flamank and Joseph be hanged until they were dead and commuting Audley's sentence from hanging, drawing and quartering to beheading. As he was drawn through the streets from the Tower to Tyburn, upside-down on his hurdle, Michael Joseph gloried in what he had done and boasted 'that he should have a name perpetual and a fame permanent and immortal'. Audley was executed on Tower Hill, wearing 'coat-armour upon him of paper, all to-torn'. The three heads were set up on Tower Bridge. The four quarters of Flamank's body were nailed to the four gates of London and Joseph's were sent down to the west country to be exhibited as a warning.

These three executions were the end of the bloodshed. Other prisoners – and there were many taken that day – were sold off at a shilling or more each, the purchaser to recover his profit before releasing the prisoner. A series of Commissions was set up to inquire into, settle, punish and pardon rebellion, and it seemed for the moment as if all was over, leaving the Cornish sadder, wiser and poorer, paying fines instead of just taxes.

The surviving rebels tramped back to Cornwall and Roger Whalley, Sir Richard Nanfan's turbulent servant, who had been fighting for once on the side of the law, went home as well. He did not find peace there: one Sunday in August, as he was coming virtuously from church in Padstow, he was set upon by John Tresyny, who had been one of Michael Joseph's captains, and by some of Lord Audley's servants. They beat him up and then left him, bruised and breathless, and set off to meet a ship which put in at Whitesand Bay, near Land's End. From the ship stepped a new leader – a new focus for Cornish discontents: Perkin Warbeck.

10 End of a Pretender

James IV had been finding Warbeck an increasing embarrassment but had scruples about handing him over to the English. Apart from the pressure exerted on him by the Spanish ambassador, de Ayala (a sporting bishop who had joined James on a border raid and got his bodyguard killed in the fun), there was also an English embassy on the way to offer him peace and King Henry's eldest daughter, Margaret. It would be a good thing to be honourably rid of Warbeck before he could be asked to abandon him. News of the Cornish rising came as a godsend. Warbeck could sail to Ireland, raise an army there and then join the Cornish, attacking Henry from the south while James attacked from the north. On a wave of Stewart optimism Warbeck and his wife were wafted to the coast where they embarked with thirty followers on the appropriately-named ship *Cuckoo*, and sailed for Cork in July.

At Cork he was joined by John Atwater the Mayor, an old friend from the days of his earliest visit to Ireland, but the rest of the Irish had had enough of Pretenders and refused to join or help him. Cork was a centre for trade with Cornwall, chiefly using the port of Padstow, and news of the Cornish defeat at Blackheath must have reached Ireland by the time Warbeck came there. Even so, Warbeck sailed for Cornwall – where else could he go? The whole continent was closed to him by the tight wall of Henry's diplomacy. Even the Irish Sea was a place of danger: during the crossing Warbeck's ship was surrounded by four ships from Waterford and he had to hide ignominiously in a wine-barrel while Henry's men searched for him. They failed to find him and on 7 September he reached Whitesand Bay, where John Tresyny and others met him and pledged him their allegiance. Leaving his wife in safety at St Michael's Mount he marched quickly to Bodmin, proclaimed himself King Richard IV, and within a few days had between three and four thousand men following his two standards – one showing a boy escaping from a tomb and the other a boy jumping out of the mouth of a wolf.

According to Henry his following included 'not one gentleman' but in fact there were a few of the lesser gentry in his force, as well as a few yeomen. Most of them, however, were copyholders or landless men, brave and hardy but 'for the most part naked men' — a description implying not exposure but a shortage of arms and armour. Experience had taught them not to march straight across England, and they decided to attack Exeter, hoping to turn it into a fortified base. They moved east from Bodmin and were met by Sir Piers Edgcumbe, who had hastily raised a posse to oppose them. But his posse joined the rebels and they marched on, Sir Piers racing indignantly ahead of them to take refuge in Exeter and warn the garrison of the coming attack.

Henry heard of the new threat at Woodstock, a manor he often visited in the summer. This time there was no army ready to throw into the field against the rebels, but he sent Daubeney to move west, gathering an army as he went, and ordered Lord Willoughby de Broke (the Sir Robert Willoughby who had brought Princess Elizabeth and the earl of Warwick to the Tower after Bosworth) to take ship and make sure Warbeck could not escape by sea.

At one o'clock on Sunday, 17 September, Warbeck reached Exeter and drew his men up outside the gates, where they stood for two hours while he demanded that the city surrender. Edward Courtenay, earl of Devon, who commanded the defences, closed the gates and lowered messengers by ropes from the walls to summon help. With him inside the city were his son, Lord William Courtenay — husband of one of the Queen's sisters — and a number of other knights and gentlemen.

Exeter is on the east of the river and its western gate was clearly impregnable, so the rebels concentrated their attack on the north and east. Realising that the gates alone could not hold, the defenders piled firewood against them and constructed trenches and ramparts behind them. That afternoon the rebels made a partial attack on the north gate, where they were held back with no great difficulty. Their main attack was on the east gate, which they broke down. They forced their way as far as Castle Street, but then the earl and his son rushed up from Blackfriars and fell on their left flank. There was a grim, hand-to-hand struggle and the rebels were slowly forced out of the city. The garrison did not try to replace the gate, but kept fires burning there all night, to discourage and reveal any attempt to rush it in the darkness.

Next morning the attack was renewed, chiefly to the north. By this time, however, the city's guns had been moved (probably, in the past ten years, the citizens had come to assume that they could only be attacked by a foreign force, coming up the river, and had neglected their landward defences). The guns were now trained on the attackers and as soon as they opened fire Warbeck seems to have given up. He treated with the garrison, who agreed to allow his army to go without pursuit or harassment. The earl, who had been wounded in the arm by an arrow, later told the King that his men were asleep on their feet, too tired for pursuit. He also reported that twenty rebels had been killed.

The rebels went to Cullompton and then turned north to Taunton, some of them slipping away home as they travelled. They reached Taunton on 20 September. Meanwhile Lord Daubeney was levying the men of South Wales, Gloucester, Wiltshire, Hampshire, Somerset and Dorset, and marching to intercept Warbeck. He gathered a sizeable force, which included Sir Rhys ap Thomas, the Welshman who had first welcomed Henry when he landed in 1485, and also the young duke of Buckingham, son of the duke who had tried to overthrow Richard III in 1483. Not far away the King was approaching with more men, passing the evening before what might have been a battle in gaming with his attendant lords – and losing £12 to them.

Towards midnight on 21 September Warbeck heard that Daubeney had reached Glastonbury. He slipped away with sixty followers (they may have been all the mounted men in his army) and galloped off towards Southampton to find a ship. Once again, as at Deal and as on James's border raid, he could not face the fact of blood being shed in his cause.

Once he was gone his army dissolved. Before the last of them fled a group of seamen met the provost of Glasney, Sir John Oby, whose severe exactions had first sparked off rebellion in the heart of Michael Joseph. They took him to Taunton and tore him to pieces in the market place.

Warbeck reached the coast to find that the seas were held by

Lord Willoughby and there was no escape. Five hundred of Daubeney's men pursued him and rounded up most of his followers. He himself managed to reach sanctuary at Beaulieu. With him were his chief councillors, and their rank shows how the captains and the kings had departed, falling away as Henry's diplomacy and growing stature made country after country abandon him. He had ridden into Antwerp with the Holy Roman Emperor. He rode into Beaulieu abbey with John Heron, bankrupt merchant of London, Edward Skelton, and Nicholas Ashley, scrivener. They threw themselves on the King's mercy and were taken to him at Taunton (no other Tudor sovereign ever travelled so far into the wild west of their dominions). Warbeck's wife was brought there with all honour and he made a full and public confession of his imposture in front of her and all the court. Then she was sent quietly to the Queen's household and her husband travelled slowly, as a show-piece, to London.

Henry moved from Taunton to Exeter, entering it in triumph on 7 October and taking part in the feasting and celebrations of the victors. He stayed at the house of the Cathedral Treasurer and eight of the sixteen trees in front of it were cut down to give him a clear view of a great concourse of rebels who were brought, each with a halter round his neck, to cry for mercy and pardon. A few ringleaders were executed and the rest pardoned. They threw away their halters, cried 'God save the King', and then set off to walk home and wait for the King's commissioners to come and fine them.

Henry returned to London and his appointed commissioners travelled from there to Cornwall to exact the penalty of rebellion twice in one year. First they fined the heads of monastic houses and boroughs. Then each of Cornwall's nine hundreds was fined. Then each parish. By the time they had finished, Cornwall was stunned and penniless. It was another fifty years, with the coming of the Reformation, before it stirred again.

Henry entered London without pomp or triumph, 'saying that he had not gained a worthy victory, having been against such a base crew as those Cornish men'. This was in keeping with his studied indifference to Warbeck throughout his career. He had always spoken of him as 'the French lad' and when he was giving an ambassador an account of the raid James IV made on England in 1496, he did not even mention that Warbeck was with him – and the ambassador was too much in awe of him to ask!

But he was not indifferent to the value of public opinion. On 27 November Warbeck publicly repeated his confession and then went through the city to the Tower. Behind him in chains walked one of his followers who had been sergeant farrier to the King. As a member of the King's household he was doubly guilty of treason and he and another of Henry's followers were hanged at Tyburn.

Warbeck, as a foreigner, was not a traitor and was soon released into a light arrest. He was allowed to associate with his wife but not to sleep with her. The King provided for him and as upstarts went in a bloodthirsty age he had done rather well for himself.

But for his restless imagination. Within a few months he was dreaming dreams again and on 9 June 1498 he stole away from the two warders who slept near him, climbed out of a window in Westminster Palace and escaped. Henry closed the roads and Warbeck took refuge in sanctuary again – at the Carthusian monastery at Sheen – near the fire-blackened ruins of Sheen Palace which had burned down earlier in the year and which Henry was rebuilding and rechristening Richmond Palace.

This time there were no half-measures. A platform was set up on barrels in Westminster Hall and stocks placed on them. There Warbeck stood all morning and there he repeated his confession. Next Monday a platform was set up in Cheapside, outside the King's Head, and Warbeck stood there in the stocks from ten in the morning until three in the afternoon, again repeating his confession. Then he was put in a cell in the Tower where, according to de Puebla, the Spanish ambassador, 'He sees neither sun nor moon'.

De Puebla had a close personal interest in Warbeck. Years before, in 1487, when Henry had been a new, insecure King, seeking anxiously for foreign allies, his chief enemy had been France and he had approached Spain, France's natural opponent. He proposed a treaty and a royal marriage and Spain, not thinking highly of him, sent as ambassador Dr Rodrigo Gonzales de Puebla, a converted Jew from Andalusia and a doctor of civil and common law. In an age when diplomacy was carried on by aristocrats or leading churchmen, a middle-class ambassador was very small beer.

Henry took him to see his pride and joy, the baby Prince Arthur, asleep in his cot, and wanted him to take Arthur's picture home. De Puebla concluded what to Spain was a minor treaty and went home in 1489. There he stayed in obscurity until, in 1494, Charles VIII invaded Italy and the English alliance suddenly became important to Spain. De Puebla was taken off the shelf, dusted down and sent back to England with instructions to bring her into the Holy League and make sure that Prince Arthur did marry Princess Catherine of Aragon.

De Puebla's position in the world depended entirely on his position as a successful ambassador – and all he ever achieved was position: his salary was always in arrears and from 1494 until his death soon after Henry's he lived in England, short of money, undignified, but shrewd and skilled. He was a figure of fun at the English court. He lived at an inn of low reputation, eating at the common table and striking up friendships with apprentices who came there to eat or drink. His landlord used the protection of the ambassador's name to cheat his clients. He was always cadging free meals at court – once the Queen asked him if his master did not provide him with food. On another occasion the King asked why de Puebla was coming to see him. A courtier said, 'To eat', and the King joined in the general laughter.

But behind the ridicule there grew up a genuine friendship between Henry and de Puebla, who may have quite enjoyed his position as the butt of the King's wit. An affection and trust developed between the ridiculous representative of the great power and the shrewd King of the little one, so that visiting Spaniards accused de Puebla of representing English interests to Spain rather than Spanish interests in England. He, for his part, was for ever writing home to explain how clever, successful and indispensable he was, and how necessary and urgent the marriage was, and it was he who persuaded Spain to send de Ayala to Scotland to induce James IV to disown Warbeck.

Now he wrote home to say that Warbeck had been put in a cell 'where he sees neither sun nor moon'. Two months later, in

August, the bishop of Cambrai in the Low Countries visited Henry and asked to see Warbeck – one of the many rumours about him had once said that Warbeck was the son of Margaret of Burgundy and the bishop. De Puebla was there when Warbeck was produced and reported that he was 'so much changed that I, and all other persons there, believe that his life will be very short. He must pay for what he has done.'

At the same time de Puebla was for ever urging Henry to free himself of all embarrassments which might make Ferdinand and Isabella dubious about marrying their daughter to the Prince of Wales. The chief embarrassment was the insecurity of the Tudor dynasty. When the marriage was first suggested, the Spanish tone had been condescending. 'Bearing in mind what happens every day to the Kings of England,' said the Spanish ambassadors, 'it is surprising that Ferdinand and Isabella should dare to give their daughter at all.' The years had made Henry a more convincing King, but he ruled a turbulent people and there was still the rise of Pretender after Pretender to be reckoned with.

The ghost of the white rose still walked the land. In February 1499 an Augustinian friar called Patrick took up with Ralph Wilford, son of a London cordwainer, and set him up as earl of Warwick. The affair was over almost as soon as it began – Wilford was hanged and Patrick imprisoned – but it must have seemed to Henry that under every stone lurked a Pretender. If such an unlikely young man could put himself forward, what member of his generation could not think himself eligible? Simnel was happy and peaceful. But if Warbeck pined away and died all Europe would say he had been poisoned. As long as Warwick lived a prisoner people would plot his escape as abbot Sante had done, or pretend that he had escaped as Simnel and Wilford had done.

Ferdinand and Isabella expressed their concern at the chanciness of the situation. Henry's hard-won position could be made to seem dubious by an infinite succession of cordwainers' sons, each of whom would be a reminder of the half-forgotten shakiness of his claim to the throne. He was on the brink of crowning his life's work by marrying his son to undoubted royalty and he lived on a house built on sand.

All through March he was troubled. He heard a sermon every

day during Lent. He consulted Master William Peronus, an astrologer, several times. He sent for a priest who had foretold the deaths of Edward IV and Richard III, but all he learned was that his life would be in danger the whole year and that 'there are two parties, of very different political creeds, in the land'. De Ayala, the sporting Spanish bishop, who had been sent to London by James IV to help with the peace negotiations, wrote home to say that Henry had aged 'so much during the past two weeks that he seems to be twenty years older'.

And so, some time in the spring or early summer, Henry seems to have taken action for his son's unblemished inheritance. Being Henry, he probably acted silently. The earl of Oxford, who was Constable of the Tower and one of the leaders of the Council, may well have been urging action on him. Master John Digby, Lieutenant or Marshal of the Tower, must have been involved, as the jailers were in his service (Oxford was the great lord who held the nominal office: Digby was the official who did the work).

The people they were moving against were Perkin Warbeck, lying ill in a dark cell – his wild, foolish behaviour had courted death several times and nobody would have any qualms about him – and the young earl of Warwick. He was twenty-four years old. His mother and brother had died when he was small – some servants were executed on a charge of poisoning them – and his father, 'false, fleeting, perjured Clarence', brother to Edward IV, had been sent to the Tower and murdered – drowned in a butt of Malmsey – when Warwick was eight. Thereafter he and his sister had been brought up by their uncle, Richard of Gloucester, with his own son, Edward. Richard became King in 1483 and his son died a year later. Richard thought of making Warwick his heir (he was next in line of succession) but chose Lincoln instead, and shut Warwick up in Sheriff Hutton castle in Yorkshire. From the age of nine, therefore, he had been a prisoner. Polydore Vergil, the historian who came to England two years after Warwick died, said that he was simple – 'he could not tell a goose from a capon'. Whether that was why Richard shut him away or whether he became simple through years of confinement is impossible to say.

His confinement in the Tower would not have been like Warbeck's. He was a nobleman, accused of no crime, held in some comfort with attendants who were servants as much as they were jailers. The Tower was a bustling place: palace, prison, armoury, ordnance-store, administrative centre, menagerie, mint and show-piece. Tower Green must have been crossed and recrossed by officials and clerks, by the royal alchemist and the chaplain as well as by the garrison and the occasional state procession winding its way out of the great gate to the City – and from time to time the stern little procession leading to the block or the gallows.

In such a busy, gossiping place Warwick grew to manhood, the innocent victim of his birth. Had times been quiet, and no Pretenders taken his name, he might have lived his life out undisturbed – might even have eventually been released. But times were not quiet. Someone (probably Digby, the Lieutenant of the Tower) moved Warbeck to a cell underneath Warwick's chamber. Among the jailers who guarded him was Thomas Astwood, who had been convicted of treason at the Stanley trials four years before, and reprieved because of his youth. Also among the jailers was one called Cleymound, who seems to have been an agent-provocateur. Astwood, being given a chance to plot, plotted. Cleymound joined in and kept Digby in touch with what was going on.

There were other Yorkist prisoners in the Tower. John Atwater, who had been mayor of Cork, had come to England with Warbeck, and he and his son were involved. And John Taylor, whose letter from Rouen to England in 1490 had been the first stirring of the Warbeck story, was a recent arrival. He had been seized by the French government and handed over to Henry in July 1499. The Milanese ambassador had written home describing this evidence of the inexorable length of Henry's arm and saying, 'This thing will be held in great account by his Majesty; much more than 100,000 crowns, as the English may say, "Whither shall I go then from thy spirit, or whither shall I flee from thy presence?"'

Atwater, his son, and John Taylor were involved in the plot. So was a group of jailers – Strangewish, Blowet, Long Roger and Girdeler – as well as Astwood and Cleymound. The conspirators' 'outside men' were Thomas Mashborough, sometime bowyer to King Edward IV, and Finch and Proud, citizens of London. The plot itself was confused and unreal. The authorities allowed it to mature for a time and then pounced. They charged Warwick, Astwood and Cleymound with having 'confederated and agreed that the earl should assume the royal dignity and elect himself King, and falsely and traiterously depose, deprive and slay the King'. Warwick was also alleged to have plotted to seize the Tower and carry away the jewels from the King's treasury; to issue a proclamation promising 12d a day to anyone who joined him; to set fire to the gunpowder stored in the Tower, and then to escape beyond the seas in the confusion and bide his time to dethrone the King. He was also alleged to have planned 'to set him (Perkin) at large and constitute him, the said Perkin, to be King and Governor of England'.

The discrepancies in these allegations suggest a group of individualists, each letting his imagination run wild, all having marvellous but discordant ideas. Clearly there was no single leading intelligence dominating them. Equally clearly, all the evidence has been angled to suggest that Warwick was the ringleader – it would be natural for the general public hearing the story to assume that in any gathering the man of rank would be the leader – but the character of the evidence and what little we know of Warwick makes his dominance incredible. He probably entered into the schoolboy side of the plot – he was said to have knocked on the floor of his chamber, to have sent Warbeck documents by Cleymound, and finally – on 4 August – to have made a hole in the floor of his chamber and to have called down to Warbeck, 'How goes it with you? Be of good cheer. Perkin, be of good cheer and comfort.' The words sound genuine enough – if one were making up the dialogue of a master-conspirator, one would do better than that! He was also said to have given Cleymound a wooden image as a token, with which Cleymound won over a clerk called Thomas Ward to the conspiracy, and to have given Cleymound a cloak and velvet jacket. Cleymound promised to give Warbeck a letter from 'one James, a clerk of Flanders' who may have been someone known to the authorities through Henry's intelligencers and mentioned to give Cleymound credibility in Warbeck's eyes.

It was a plot which must have involved much coming and going of corrupt jailers between Warwick, Warbeck, Warbeck's ex-followers and the 'outside men', and it continued through August, September and early November. Then, on 12 November, the Chief Justice, Fineux, told the Council 'of certain treasons conspired of Edward, naming himself of Warwick, and Perkin and other within the Tower: which intended as it appeareth by the confessions of the said Edward and other to have deposed and destroyed the King's person and his blood. And over that the said Edward intended to have been King: And first to have holpen Perkin to the crown if he had been King Edward's son and else to have had it himself. It is determined by all the said judges that they have done treason and deserved death. It is thereupon demanded by the King's Grace what is to be done herein, whether process of law pass upon them, or else that nothing be done further upon the same treasons. All the said Councillors and every of them by himself adviseth, counselleth and prayeth that not only process but execution of justice be also had, of not only Perkin but also of the said Edward and other offenders.'

In important state trials at this time the real trial was an inquiry conducted by a sub-committee of the Council in private and fairly informally. If they decided to proceed to public trial the accused would automatically be convicted and sentenced: the public trial was largely a formality. By 12 November, therefore, the inquiry was complete and the accused condemned in all but formality. Warwick was tried in Westminster Hall before a court presided over by the earl of Oxford (created Lord High Steward for the occasion) and consisting of the duke of Buckingham, the earls of Northumberland, Kent, Surrey and Essex, sixteen barons (including Lord Bergavenny) and Sir John Kendal, the ointment-buying grand prior of the Order of St John of Jerusalem. Warwick pleaded guilty and no evidence was given.

Warbeck and Atwater, the mayor of Cork, were drawn from the Tower to Tyburn in the usual manner – 'drawn to the place of execution from their prison, as being not worthy any more to tread upon the face of the earth whereof they were made; also for that they have been retrograde to nature, therefore are they to be drawn backward at a horse-tail. And whereas God hath made the head of man the highest and most supreme part, as being his chief grace and ornament, they must be drawn with their heads declining downward, and lying so near the ground as may be, being thought unfit to take benefit of the common air.' At the end of this long, grisly journey (Tyburn was where Marble Arch is today and Tudor streets were bumpy) Warbeck stood 'on a small scaffold' and confessed for the last time that he was not King Edward's son. He asked forgiveness of God and the King and then he and Atwater were executed (but mercifully – they were hanged until dead before being disembowelled and quartered). Warbeck's confession was quickly printed and circulated. The two heads were set on London Bridge and their bodies were buried at the Augustine Friars'.

Warwick was the next to die. He was beheaded five days later, on 28 November, between two and three in the afternoon, and his head was not set up on view. His body was taken, on the next tide, up the river to Bisham Abbey in Berkshire, where he was buried, at the King's expense, with his ancestors.

On 4 December Blowet and Astwood were executed as Warbeck and Atwater had been, and their heads set on Tower Bridge. The other conspirators were reprieved and sent to prison. Cleymound alone was never brought to trial – which is the best reason for thinking he was the agent provocateur.

Warbeck's wife, the Lady Catherine Gordon, remained at court, where her charm is said to have won her 'the name of the White Rose, which had been given to her husband's false title'. Eleven years later she married, and when her second husband died she married again – each time to a gentleman of the King's bedchamber. The King was generous in giving her a good allowance and a home of her own.

As for her first husband, Francis Bacon, in his history, summed up Warbeck's career as 'one of the longest plays of that kind that hath been in memory, and might perhaps have had another end, if he had not met with a King both wise, stout and fortunate'.

11 Master in his House

The years 1500 and 1501 saw Henry's reign at its zenith. He had been fifteen years a King and each year made his throne more secure. His eldest son – the apple of his father's eye – was already at work with his own court and officials governing Wales and the western marches. He and Catherine of Aragon had already been married by proxy, with fat, middle-aged Dr de Puebla standing in for the bride. Negotiations were in hand for the marriage of Princess Margaret with James IV of Scotland. In 1500 Henry and Queen Elizabeth went to Calais where they met the Archduke Philip for several days of diplomacy, dancing and tournaments. England was prosperous at home and at peace with her neighbours.

Within his family, too, Henry was happy. He was never a demonstrative man but he had a real affection for both his brilliant mother and his quiet queen. His third son, Prince Edmund, died in 1500 at the age of two, but there were two sons and two daughters left. Arthur was a slight, serious boy and Henry a stocky, rosy-cheeked child, more like his uncle Edward IV than his father. He was not as scholarly as Arthur but, when Erasmus visited the royal nursery in 1499, he was able to receive and entertain him correctly, and to write him a schoolboy note in Latin – he was eight years old, and seems to have taken his education in a princely manner: enough to shine but not enough to weigh him down.

The King's family life can be traced in the pages of his meticulous accounts. It was a musical family:

for flutes in a case	3.10.–
for a lute for my lady Mary (his younger daughter)	13.4
to the princess's string minstrels at Westminster	2. –.–
to a woman that singeth with the fiddle	2.–
to the Welsh harper	6.8
to the trumpets that blow when the King come over the water	3.4
to the children for singing in the garden	3.4

They read – Henry bought many books and manuscripts and gave considerable sums to poets. They hunted, hawked, jousted, shot at the butts, enjoyed cock-fights and bear-baiting and gambled on chess, dice, cards, archery and tennis. In one wild game the King lost tennis balls to the value of 3/–. He bought a lion for £2.13.4 and a leopard for £13.6.8. He enjoyed May games, play-actors and morris dancers:

to one that joculed before the King	10.–
to a tumbler upon a rope	3.4
to a fellow for eating coals	6.8
to Ringley Abbot of Misrule (at Twelfth Night)	5. –.–
to the Scottish boy with the beard	10.–
to the little maiden that danceth	12. –.–

As he moved about the country his subjects would greet him with presents, and be rewarded:

to a mariner that brought an eagle	6.8
to Clement for a nightingale	1. –.–
to a woman for a nest of leverets	3.4
to beer drunken at the farmer's house	1.–
to a poor woman for cherries and strawberries	1.8
for two glasses of water	5.–
to the reapers in the way of reward	2
to the smith of Richmond for a little clock	13.4

When the King's deer ate a poor man's corn near Woking, he paid compensation. The Keeper's daughter at Westminster was bound apprentice with money given by the King, and he tipped a woman who brought him a red rose. A cook called John Van Delf was paid £38.1.4 for garnishing a salad – at a time when a man could call himself a gentleman on a cash income of £10 a year, it must have been a notable salad.

A shadow on the horizon came with the sudden flight of the earl of Suffolk, younger brother of the dead earl of Lincoln, who went to the Emperor Maximilian and set up as the last of the Pretenders. But that trouble could be forgotten as the whole of southern England prepared to welcome the Princess Catherine of Aragon.

She arrived at Plymouth on 2 October 1501. She was almost

sixteen years old, sturdily built with red-gold hair and a fair complexion. She was thoroughly trained in all the duties and graces of royalty and from the first attracted the liking of a nation which regarded foreigners with suspicion. The nobility and gentry of the west country crowded to greet and entertain her as she rode through the autumn countryside, escorted by Lord Willoughby de Broke.

It was officially planned that Henry and Arthur should meet her at Lambeth, but there was a tradition under which a royal bridegroom was supposed to be impatient to see his bride, and to gatecrash her apartments on her journey. James IV was to do so when Princess Margaret travelled north to marry him in 1503 – it was a tradition honoured even by Napoleon centuries later.

Accordingly, Henry met Arthur, come home from the Welsh marches, and they rode together to meet her at Dogmersfield. They were intercepted by de Ayala, the Spanish ambassador, who ought to have been in Scotland but found England more comfortable, and who was enjoying manifold opportunities to infuriate the regular ambassador, de Puebla, with his easy aristocratic insolence. De Ayala carried a message from the princess's escort: a Spanish princess must not be seen unveiled, even by her future husband, until the wedding ceremony was completed.

Henry called a hasty Council on horseback in a sodden field (by now it was early November), concluded that Catherine was already an English, not a Spanish princess, and rode on masterfully, outdistancing his son and his escort, to brush aside Catherine's household and meet her face to face. She was, after all, the great diplomatic triumph of his reign: he was impatient to see that she was worth all the trouble he had taken. They met briefly; they met again formally when Arthur caught up with his father, and Henry was satisfied.

The wedding was spectacular and magnificent. The bride was led down the aisle of St Paul's by ten-year-old Prince Henry; London streets were elaborately decorated with triumphal arches and allegorical scenes; a conduit outside the cathedral flowed with wine; the bells rang, the people cheered, the bride and groom were riotously bedded at Baynard's Castle, and next day everyone took his hangover to the tournament at Westminster.

The tournament was more a matter of aristocratic amateur dramatics than of fighting but it was greatly applauded – everyone fought well, nobody got hurt, and all the right people won, and more dramatic, symbolic and allegorical entertainments filled the subsequent days of festivity; the wedding celebrations went on for more than a week. Catherine may have been impressed by four monstrous beasts – a golden lion, a silver lion, a hart and an elk, which were worked by eight men, two hidden inside each animal. They appeared every day – as they had done at every royal occasion for years, freshened up from time to time with a lick of paint. There was dancing as well as pageantry, jousting and feasting. Catherine danced herself and Prince Henry jumped about so energetically that he eventually took off his splendid doublet and danced in his shirt.

When the celebrations were over there was a brief debate in the Council as to whether, when Arthur returned to Wales, Catherine should accompany him or stay at court with Queen Elizabeth until she was a little older. It was decided that she should go with her husband, and the two of them rode away along the muddy December roads to Ludlow castle, where Sir Rhys ap Thomas (King Henry's 'father Rhys') greeted them at the head of a succession of Welsh lords, and gave Catherine his son, Griffith ap Rhys, to be her gentleman usher and Welsh interpreter.

For three months Arthur ruled his court in the west and Henry, in his larger court near London, could think with satisfaction of the success his life's work had achieved. Then the sweating sickness (which seems to have been some sort of deadly influenza) struck Catherine down and kept her for many weeks in her bed. While she was struggling with the high fever, Arthur fell ill as well. She was a sturdy girl, he was a delicate boy; on 2 April he died.

'Immediately after his death,' wrote the chronicler Leland, 'Sir Richard Poole his Chamberlain, with other of his Council, wrote and sent letters to the King and Council to Greenwich, where his Grace and the Queen lay, and certified them of the Prince's departure. The which Council discreetly sent for the King's ghostly father, a Friar Observant, to whom they showed this most sorrowful and heavy tidings, and desired him in his best manner to show it to the King. He in the morning of the Tuesday following, somewhat before the time accustomed, knocked at the King's chamber door; and when the King understood it was his Confessor, he commanded to let him in.

'The Confessor then commanded all those there present to avoid, and after due salutation began to say, "Si bona de manu dei suscipimus, mala autem quare non sustineamus?" And so showed his Grace that his dearest son was departed to God. When his Grace understood that sorrowful heavy tidings, he sent for the Queen, saying that he and his Queen would take the painful sorrow together.

'After that she was come and saw the King her lord, and that natural and painful sorrow, as I have heard say, she with full great and constant comfortable words besought his Grace, that he would first, after God, remember the weal of his own noble person, the comfort of his realm, and of her. She then said that my Lady his mother had never no more children but him only, and that God by his grace had ever preserved him, and brought him where that he was. Over that, how that God had left him yet a fair prince, two fair princesses; and that God is where he was, and that we are both young enough: and that the prudence and wisdom of his Grace sprung over all Christendom, so that it should please him to take this accordingly thereunto. Then the King thanked her of her good comfort.

'After that she was departed and came to her own chamber, natural and motherly remembrance of that great loss smote her so sorrowful to the heart, that those that were about her were fain to send for the King to comfort her. Then his Grace of true and gentle faithful love, in good haste came and relieved her, and showed her how wise council she had given him before; and he for his part would thank God for his son, and would she do in likewise.'

So they comforted each other, as Catherine lay ill at Ludlow and Griffith ap Rhys rode his black-draped horse at the head of the funeral procession, carrying Arthur's banner reversed. They travelled roads so bad that they had to find oxen to drag the coffin on its carriage, until the sodden procession, with its eighty torches flattened by the wind, reached Worcester cathedral and the Prince of Wales was buried.

Henry and Elizabeth had a son and two daughters living – all healthy and a very fair survival rate for the time. Moreover, as Elizabeth had pointed out, 'We are both young enough.' She was thirty-five and he was forty-four years old. There could never be another Arthur, but there could be more sons – and it was sons who mattered. Matilda was the only Queen regnant in English history, and no one wanted to repeat the experiment.

Meanwhile politics could not wait on grief, either in England or in Spain. The marriage was the seal on an alliance: what was to be done to repair the damage? Spain, preparing to confront France and plagued by the unreliability of her other ally, Maximilian, took no time to draw breath before taking action. Within twenty-four hours of hearing the news, Ferdinand and Isabella had an ambassador on his way to England carrying two documents for King Henry. The first, to be shown at once, was a formal demand that Henry restore to Catherine that part of her dowry already paid over, that he give her her dower rights to a third of the revenues of Wales, Chester and Cornwall, and that he restore her to her parents in Spain. The second, to be held in reserve and used at discretion, authorised the ambassador to arrange for Catherine, instead of coming home, to marry Prince Henry.

King Henry was fully aware that Spain needed him at this moment more than he needed Spain. He did not for one moment think of complying with Spain's first demand. Instead he spun out the negotiations into an infinity of complications, with the Council arguing over the Latin grammar in minor clauses of treaties they had no intention of taking seriously and Henry explaining that he could not move while his Council was divided – he was very good at convincing foreign ambassadors that his hands were tied and that he could do nothing without consent of Council. And every moment of argument and delay gave him more time to see how the contest between Spain and France would go, and whether the Spanish alliance was worthwhile any more.

Henry was all his life a gambler – a chess-player and a card-player – and diplomatic poker was his element. In Ferdinand he had a worthy opponent – the trickiest monarch in Europe – and he held slightly better cards than Ferdinand.

While he played the game through the summer of 1502, Queen

Elizabeth was pregnant for the first time in four years – perhaps there would be another son to buttress the dynasty. The child was due early in February and the place chosen for the birth was the Tower. On 26 January the Queen went there by barge from Richmond, to the rooms which had been prepared for her and where an English and a French nurse were waiting. The procedure for her confinements had been laid down by Margaret Beaufort at the birth of Prince Arthur sixteen years before: 'Her Highness's pleasure being understood as to what chamber it may please her to be delivered in, the same be hung with rich cloth or arras, sides, roof, windows and all, except one window, which must be hanged so that she have light when it pleases her' – all these hangings were needed to keep out every possible draught, so that the good, stuffy, smelly fug necessary to the health of new-born babies and their mothers could be satisfactorily built up.

The Queen took communion at a solemn mass and then went in great state to her apartments. There she stayed for a time in an ante-room where everyone was served with sweet wines and comfits. Then she bade farewell to her lords and officers and went into her chamber, where 'women are to be made all manner of officers, butlers, sewers and pages; receiving all needful things at the chamber door'. There also would be waiting the cradle first made for Prince Arthur – 'a little cradle of tree, a yard and a quarter long, and twenty-two inches broad, in a frame set forth by painter's craft, superbly furnished with cloth of gold, ermine fur and crimson velute'.

On 2 February Princess Catherine was born. At first all seemed well, but within a few days the Queen became seriously ill, probably with puerperal fever. Henry sent a messenger hurrying to Kent to fetch Dr Aylsworth, who had a high reputation, but she died on her birthday, 11 February. Princess Catherine 'tarried but a small season after her mother', her only mark in history being the purchase of four yards of flannel, at a shilling a yard, to keep her from the perilous draughts.

> If worship might have kept me, I had not gone.
> If wit might have me saved, I needed not fear.
> If money might have holp, I lacked none.
> But oh good God, what vaileth all this gear?

When death is come, thy mighty messenger,
Obey we must, there is no remedy,
Me hath he summoned, and lo now here I lie.

Adieu mine own dear spouse, my worthy lord,
The faithful love that did us both combine
In marriage and peaceable concord,
Into your handes here I clean resign
To be bestowed upon your children and mine;
Erst were you father, and now ye must supply
The mother's part also, for lo now here I lie.

So wrote young Thomas More in his lament for the Queen. King
Henry, having given detailed orders for the funeral, 'privily withdrew to a solitary place, and would no man should resort unto
him'. He did not go to see her buried.

12 The Last Pretender

When the earl of Lincoln died at the battle of Stoke, he left alive behind him four brothers: Edmund, Humphrey, William and Richard. Of these four boys only Humphrey was to live a life unclouded by his closeness to the Yorkist claim: he became a country rector and died in peaceful obscurity in 1513, at the age of thirty-nine.

The other boys were brought up in the normal expectations of nobility at that time. In particular Edmund – who was nearly ten years younger than his elder brother – received especial notice from King Henry and was frequently at court. His father's death made him briefly Henry's ward. The King had decided that the family estates, diminished as they were by the forfeiture of those settled on Lincoln, were insufficient to support a dukedom, and Edmund celebrated his twenty-first birthday by agreeing to surrender the dukedom and be known as the earl of Suffolk. Henry wanted as few dukes as possible in his kingdom.

It was an arrangement which appeared to be agreeable to everyone, but it lodged at the back of young Suffolk's mind as a grievance and an affront to his pride of family. For the time being, however, he took his place as one of the leading noblemen of the new generation, 'stout and bold of courage and of wit rash and heady', taking his part in ceremonial, administration, tournaments and all the other duties and pleasures of his place. In 1497 he was to have been one of the leaders in the army raised to fight the Scots, and it was he who was called from his bed at Ewelme to go and hold Staines bridge against the Cornish – and who went there with Lord Bergavenny's shoes in his saddlebag.

Lord Bergavenny alternated, throughout the reign, between honour and disgrace. He was a busy and active member of the Council, but in 1506 he spent some time in the Tower on a charge of treason resulting from his words spoken that early morning. A year later he pleaded guilty before the King's Bench to retaining 471 men for thirty months, most of the men being yeomen drawn from eighty towns and villages in mid-Kent. They were potentially a small army and he was fined the statutory amount of £5 per man per month – making up the astronomical figure of £70,650. In due course he paid £5,000 of his fine and entered into a recognisance that he would not enter Kent, Surrey, Sussex or Hampshire without the King's permission. The rest of the fine was remitted and we are left to speculate on what he had been thinking of doing with his 471 retainers.

He was not the only young nobleman to get into trouble during the reign. A few years before, in the Michaelmas term 1498, Suffolk was indicted in the King's Bench for 'slaying of a mean person'. He was pardoned, but he seems to have felt that the pardon should have come before the humiliation of the trial (as if the King could pardon someone before he was convicted) and the affair rankled deeply. Suddenly, on 1 July 1499, he left the country, a thing he had no right to do without the King's permission. It was more a tantrum than a defection, for he went only to Guisnes, a castle about six miles south of Calais, held for the King by Sir James Tyrrell, one of Richard III's old supporters now reconciled to Henry. He had crossed the seas but he remained in English territory. Henry seems to have interpreted his action as a bad case of the sulks, but he took it seriously, and made a real effort to get him to return in friendship.

Sir Richard Guildford and Richard Hatton were leaving in September on a mission to the Archduke Philip. Henry told them to break their journey at Guisnes. They were given an elaborate series of instructions, drawn up by Henry and Richard Fox (by now bishop of Durham). The matter was important enough for Fox to correct and amplify the instructions with his own hand. There were two sets of instructions. The first expressed the King's affection for Suffolk, his desire to have him home again, and his readiness to overlook his going abroad without permission. The second was much more detailed.

Guildford and Hatton, without saying they had been told to do so, were to show their first set of instructions to Suffolk, allowing him to read it and, if he wished, take it to his lodgings to study at his leisure. They were to persuade him to return home, if possible with Sir James Tyrrell. If he insisted that he would only return accompanied by Sir Richard Guildford, then – despite the importance of his embassy and although the Archduke was expecting him – Guildford was to break off his mission and bring Suffolk home. If Suffolk persisted in travelling on without the King's licence, Sir Richard was to 'take him apart and, as it were of himself and for the favour he beareth him, and as it were without the King's knowledge' to point out that the King would tell all his allies that he was a fugitive rebel, and that they were bound by treaty to seize him and return him to Henry – and Henry's allies included most of the states of Europe by this time. If, in spite of all these warnings, Suffolk 'will always keep forth his journey', Sir Richard was – again speaking as if it were his own idea – to point out that, provided Suffolk and his companions behaved, wherever they went, as true and faithful subjects of the King in word and deed, then in time to come it was likely that their friends at home would be able to persuade the King to forgive them and to receive them, allowing Suffolk 'all that he had when he departed'.

Sir Richard and Hatton were successful in their mission, and Suffolk returned to every appearance of honour and allegiance at home. When the King met the Archduke Philip at Calais in 1500, Suffolk was one of the leaders in the lighter side of events – the jousting, the dancing and the banqueting on kids, beef, venison pasties, spiced cakes, strawberries and cream and 'seven horseloads of cherries'.

At this point the ambiguous figure of Sir Robert Curzon entered the story. He had known Suffolk for some time (they rode together in the tournament when Prince Henry became duke of York). He had been in charge of the King's castle at Hammes, near Calais, and in 1499 he had asked the King's permission to go to fight against the Turks. Since he was going at his own expense, the King had no objection. Sir Robert went to war and won the admiration of Maximilian, who made him a baron of the Holy Roman Empire. While they were talking together Sir Robert mentioned the 'murders and tyrannies' of Henry VII – it was the year of the judicial murder of the earl of Warwick, and there was much bitterness about it. Maximilian, who had been Warbeck's most persistent supporter, said that 'if he might have one of King Edward's blood on his hands, he would help him to recover the crown of England and be revenged on H, or else he would spend as much money as his whole lands were in value for a whole year'. Maximilian was a great one for the talking.

Sir Robert let Suffolk know what had been said and, in August 1501, as Henry was preparing to meet Catherine of Aragon, he learnt that Suffolk and his youngest brother, Richard de la Pole, had gone to join Maximilian in the Tyrol.

Sir Robert Curzon and Suffolk were solemnly excommunicated at St Paul's cross and London exploded in gossip. Five or six nights before he absconded, Suffolk had banqueted privately with Dorset, Essex and Lord William Courtenay – was this suspicious? Knowing he was about to leave, he had told Dorset and Courtenay that he wanted each of them to have one of his horses, but they must send to collect them quickly – had they done so in time, before the King's officers arrived to take charge of the traitor's forfeited property? Just before he left, Suffolk had dined with the earl of Devon, who came to his outer gate to receive him with great reverence – were they in collusion? Would Suffolk, when he invaded, land on the earl's estates? An astrologer had prophesied that Suffolk would 'come to his desires' and Suffolk had sent to ask him 'what day would be most expedient for him to make a privy journey'.

Henry took a little time to sift the gossip – for several months sundry gentlemen were attending court with a draughty feeling round the neck. Then Suffolk's brother William was arrested and sent to the Tower where he was to live out the rest of his life, gradually rising to the position of senior prisoner and dying, unremarked, some time between spring 1538 and autumn 1540. With him went Dorset (son of the marquis left in Paris by Henry in 1485 – he had died earlier that year) and Lord William Courtenay, whose marriage had made him a cousin of Suffolk's and a brother-in-law of the Queen. Suffolk was proclaimed outlaw and he and his brothers attainted – their estates forfeit to the crown.

Sir Robert Curzon, having been excommunicated as a rebel, stayed abroad until 1506, when he returned to a full pardon and a pension of £500 a year. After his outburst of 1499, time and a better understanding of Suffolk's character may have made him appreciate Henry's qualities. Towards the end of his period abroad he may have been already reconciled to Henry and working as his agent. Certainly Henry was very well-informed about all Suffolk's movements.

Sir James Tyrrell in the castle at Guisnes was not so easy to arrest as Dorset and Courtenay had been. Sir Thomas Lovell was sent with commands that he must be taken at all costs. The garrison of Calais laid siege to Guisnes, but a long siege in country so close to France was to be avoided. Sir Thomas sent Sir James a safe-conduct, asking him to come aboard Sir Thomas's ship at Calais to discuss the situation. He came, and was told that he would be thrown overboard if he did not send his son a token, telling him to surrender the castle. His son obeyed and a group of prisoners was taken to the Tower, some to be executed (among them Sir James but not his son) and others to be imprisoned or pardoned. Before he died, Sir James set the cat among the historical pigeons for the next four hundred and fifty years by admitting that he had killed the little princes in the Tower, at the request of Richard III. Setting aside the bonus to Henry of a confession to regicide and infanticide, Sir James does seem to have been intriguing with Suffolk.

Suffolk, meanwhile, was learning how great a distance stood between Maximilian's promises and his performances. He and his followers (who included his brother Richard, his cousin Sir George Neville the Bastard, his steward Thomas Killingworth and his chaplain, Sir Walter Blesset) were made welcome and he began to call himself the duke of Suffolk and the White Rose. Maximilian explained that immediate, overt help would endanger the friendship between his son, the Archduke Philip, and Henry. Suffolk suggested that he seek his fortune elsewhere. Maximilian asked him to wait. He waited for six weeks. Maximilian offered him between three and five thousand soldiers for up to three months – a shortish time in which to overthrow a King and establish oneself in his place. Maximilian and Suffolk signed an agreement that this loan should be given. Suffolk went with letters of recommendation to get more help from the free town of Aix-la-Chapelle, leaving Killingworth to watch his interests at Maximilian's court.

While this went on Henry was not twiddling his thumbs. Maximilian had previously asked him for financial help in his perennial war against the Turks. In June 1502 Henry's ambassadors agreed that ten thousand pounds should go to Maximilian. If he agreed to expel all Henry's rebellious subjects it would be a gift: otherwise it was a loan. Maximilian, having checked that Suffolk really was in Aix-la-Chapelle, agreed to hand over all rebels, pocketed the gift, and then explained that as Aix was a free city, he could not force its citizens to expel anyone.

Instead of soldiers, Maximilian sent Suffolk a series of excuses and bright new plans. Killingworth kept pressing him, and he said he would arrange for the King of Denmark to help, and to launch the invasion of England from his territory. Several envoys to Denmark failed to set out, and Maximilian suggested to Curzon that he should reconcile Suffolk and Henry, or that he might find the French helpful. Slowly Suffolk sank into a morass of negotiation and intrigue, overshadowed by a growing mountain of debt.

1503, the year of the Queen's death, was a year of obscure plots. Overseas, Suffolk was pointing out excitedly to Maximilian that only Prince Henry stood between him and the throne. At home Walter Roberts of Cranbrook in Kent, who had taken part in Buckingham's abortive rising in 1483, sent one of his dependants, a carpenter called Alexander Symson, through the Suffolk lands to find out what support there would be for an invasion, and then over the seas to report to Suffolk. When Symson reached Aix-la-Chapelle, he found lodgings with a cobbler where Suffolk's men resorted. They took him to Sir George Neville the Bastard and a white friar whose name he did not learn, but who was probably Suffolk's chaplain. They viewed him with great suspicion and Sir George opened the conversation disconcertingly by threatening to have his ears cut off and saying he had never heard of Walter Roberts. The friar eased the situation by saying, 'I know him well enough. He is right a sad wiseman' and Symson was allowed to tell his story, after which he was 'neither evil dealt with nor evil said to' but told to get out of town by eight o'clock next morning.

He found out what he could about Suffolk's intentions and then returned home in a hoy carrying salt fish, which landed him at Erith on the Kentish bank of the Thames. At this point his statement – taken down in the Tower by the clerk of the Council –

begins to show signs of having been thought up after his arrest. According to him, he had a change of heart and, although he went home, only did so to collect his saw. He spent a night with his wife, without seeing Walter Roberts, and then, armed with his saw and a new resolution, set out to find Sir Richard Guildford and tell him the whole story. Sir Richard had been one of the leaders of the Kentish section of Buckingham's rising in 1483 and Walter Roberts had then hidden him until he could escape abroad to join Henry. As a landowner in Kent he would be the one great man of the realm well known to a Kentish carpenter.

So – according to his story – Alexander Symson went to Sutton, near Dartford, where he ran out of money and worked until he had earned two shillings. Then he moved on to Erith again, where rude hands were laid on him and he was taken to the Tower by the Erith constable and mayor with the help of five Erith citizens. Thomas Broke, one of the five citizens, deposed that on St James's day at night he was having a drink in his local pub when Symson came in and asked if he was the landlord. Broke said he was (he wasn't). Symson asked if he could trust him, for if he could he would show him a matter which would be to his profit. Broke asked what it should be. Symson said he had with him a child, James Ormond, who had been abducted from the keeping of the prior of Christ Church, Canterbury, and who 'should be a great inheritor and next unto the crown'. He asked Broke to get him a boat and promised him forty marks a year if he would help to get the child to the continent.

The child was questioned and said that Symson had promised to make him a great lord, if he did as he was told. He was one of the great Irish family – perhaps a nephew of the anglicised Lord Ormond who was a loyal member of the Council. It may be that Suffolk was trying to buy the help of the Irish Ormonds by offering them an Irish crown if they would help him to an English one.

It has been suggested that the whole conspiracy was engineered by Henry, since Walter Roberts lived on quietly as a JP – or as quietly as a man can live with three successive wives and thirty children. But the whole plot has about it the disorderly smack of nature, and it would have been beyond Henry's powers to supervise anything so woolly. Probably Sir Richard Guildford intervened to help the man who had saved his life in 1483. It may be relevant that Walter Roberts's home at Cranbrook was in central Kent, where Bergavenny was at this time retaining his 471 men.

The uncertain state of the world at this time is well reflected in a conversation held among leading officials in the castle of Calais the next year, 1504. They were loyal men, but they fell to discussing what would happen if the King were to die (in itself a treasonable subject). They had heard that he was ailing; they had read a prophecy that he would reign no longer than Edward IV, and they discussed the succession. It seemed to them to lie between the young duke of Buckingham and the earl of Suffolk, 'but none of them spake of my lord prince'. Prince Henry was thirteen at that time – in fact his father lived just long enough for him to be of an age to take the throne without dispute.

They were also worried at the vulnerability of Calais, fearing that traitors within might open the gates to traitors without – 'The King once departed and Edmund de la Pole at his liberty, and let them come into this town by the postern of the castle to the destruction of us all'. They thought 'how nigh Kent is hither, what allegiance they be of there', and they worried about the King's reluctance to believe those who spoke ill of others: 'I know that the King's highness is hard of credence in such matters . . . for how long it was ere his Grace and his Council would believe anything of untruth to be in Sir James Tyrrell.'

Seen from Calais, Suffolk looked dangerous. To him his situation was nothing so happy. Maximilian was under pressure from Henry and eventually promised to expel Suffolk, even from Aix. He wrote to the burgomaster saying that Suffolk must leave and promising to make his departure possible by sending 3,000 Rhenish florins to discharge his debts. As one would expect he did not actually go so far as to send the money, and for another year Suffolk lingered in Aix, eventually leaving his brother Richard as hostage for his debts.

He arranged to join the Duke of Saxony, but in the course of his journey fell into the hands of the Duke of Gelders, who held him virtually a prisoner for fourteen months, writing urgent, illiterate letters to Killingworth (writing was no occupation for a gentleman) all about money and his need for clothes. And Richard was writing desperately to him for help. The people of Aix were growing ugly in their demands for money and 'I am told by two people who are my friends that King H had desired the burgesses of Aix to deliver me three leagues out of the town of Aix and he will pay them. And so I am advised not to go into the street, for if I am killed in the street, King Henry will pay them their money.'

Through Killingworth, Suffolk appealed to the Archduke Philip at Brussels. Philip responded and Suffolk found himself under his protection, while the bishop of Liège at last came to Richard's help, paid off his debts and saw him safely to Hungary. In Philip's hands Suffolk had diplomatic value, but Philip had no intention of handing him over to Henry.

Here chance and the weather intervened – or as the men of that age would have said, God ended the matter. Queen Isabella had died and Philip's wife, Juana, inherited Castile. He was conscious that his father-in-law, Ferdinand of Aragon, would try to seize Castile for himself, and set sail early in January 1506 to claim his wife's kingdom.

There came a great gale which blew the bronze eagle off the spire of St Paul's. In its fall it knocked to the ground the sign of the Black Eagle tavern in Cheapside. Maximilian's arms included the black eagle and the omen was felt to point to his family. It was judged to have been fulfilled when the same gale, after nearly drowning Philip and his fleet, washed them up on the shores of England.

The Venetian ambassador found himself immobilised and in-communicado at Plymouth in a wild land where there were no roads and nobody talked English, let alone Italian, Latin or French. Philip and Queen Juana were luckier and landed near Weymouth, whence they were taken with all honour to Windsor, to be fêted and feasted and, in the most cordial manner possible, squeezed. Henry and Philip took to each other: while their courtiers danced and Princess Mary played the lute, the two men slipped away repeatedly into corners to talk. Then Henry would walk Philip to his lodgings for the night and Philip turn to walk Henry back to his, until it seemed that neither of them would ever get to bed.

At this very time Suffolk was dictating instructions to Killingworth, who was to come to negotiate a reconciliation with Henry. Suffolk was lost in a day-dream, speaking as one prince to another, calling himself the duke of Suffolk and demanding that he retain that title on his return, that he have all his property restored, and that freedom, pardon and restoration be given to his brother William and his cousin, Sir George Neville the Bastard. All these conditions fulfilled, Henry would find in Suffolk, 'on his faith as a true Christian prince', an obedient subject – if he would please rescue him from Philip.

Henry was rescuing him in his own fashion. At the end of Philip's visit on 15 March 1506, Suffolk was handed over to the English at Calais, passing the marquis of Dorset and Lord William Courtenay, who were imprisoned there, and crossing to England where, on 24 March, he was paraded through the streets of London on his way to join his brother William in the Tower. Henry had promised Philip not to execute him, and he remained in the Tower until he was beheaded by Henry's son, who had made no promise to anyone.

Killingworth struggled for a time, himself in poverty and debt, appealing to Maximilian to help both Suffolk and Richard. It was of no avail, and eventually he accepted a pardon from Henry and came home to England to hand his papers over and to fade into peace and out of history.

13 To End Alone

Prince Edmund, aged two, and Archbishop Morton, aged seventy-seven, both died in 1500. In 1501 the marquis of Dorset died. In 1502 Prince Arthur died. In 1503 the Queen and her new-born daughter died, and so did Sir Reginald Bray, who had started his career as steward to Margaret Beaufort's second husband, and ended it running the finances of the country, supervising the building of the King's two great ships, the *Regent* and the *Sovereign*, and also overseeing Henry's new chapel at Westminster.

Morton had been something of a father-figure, a man of great spiritual authority. 'In his face,' wrote Sir Thomas More, who spent two years of his childhood in Morton's household, 'did shine such an amiable reverence as was pleasant to behold, gentle in communication, yet earnest and sage. He had great delight many times with rough speech to suitors to prove, but without harm, what prompt wit and bold spirit were in every man. In his speech he was fine, eloquent and pithy. . . . In the law he had profound knowledge, in wit he was incomparable, and in memory wonderful excellent.' Bray had given the government its essential foundation of solvency and was one of the few who were able 'humbly to reprehend the King' if they thought he was acting wrongly.

These men were a great loss, and other senior members of the Council died during the next few years, though Fox and Oxford both outlived their master. Oxford lived quietly, dying in 1513 at the age of seventy. Fox retained the Privy Seal until 1516, by which time his protégé Wolsey had proved himself capable and energetic, and he could 'retire' for the last twelve years of his life – administering his diocese, founding a college at Oxford and schools at Taunton and his home town of Grantham, and teaching his clergy in 'common, plain, round English, easy to be understood' until at last, nearly blind and nearly deaf, he died. He was about eighty-two years old.

Apart from these two, there were the new men – often efficient and conscientious, but unable to share the King's memories or come close to him. He was a family man and his family also seemed to be slipping away from him. Arthur and Elizabeth were the two great losses of his life, but he must have missed Uncle Jasper, dead in 1495. His mother spent less time at court and her husband died in 1504 (at which she took a vow of chastity, being sixty-one years old). In the summer of 1503 Henry escorted his elder daughter, Margaret, part of the way north to her wedding. They stayed for a few days with Margaret Beaufort and then Surrey took Margaret on to Scotland and Henry turned back.

There were now only two children within reach: Henry and Mary. The King became obsessed with the health and welfare of his son. Instead of having a separate household, as one would expect of a royal child, he shared the King's, and the prince's room could only be reached through his father's. A Spanish ambassador reported that he was completely dominated by his father and grandmother and on public occasions spoke only to them. He took exercise near the palace, surrounded by his tutors and guardians, and was being brought up more like a girl than a future King. The ambassador was exaggerating – the prince was a sportsman and he had companions of his own age, young noblemen who were in no way sheltered or interested in scholarship.

When his wife died the King was forty-six years old – a greater age then than now, but not one to turn a man into a slippered pantaloon. He was a middle-aged man with only one heir. From the point of view of the other powers, he was the most eligible man in Europe. Matrimonial negotiations started as soon as the news could cross the Channel.

Henry's first suggestion was his daughter-in-law, Catherine. She was eligible, her dowry was partly paid, and she was not quite thirty years younger than himself. The idea hung for a moment in the air, to be immediately extinguished by Isabella of Castile. She was not shocked by it, or afraid the Pope might withhold the necessary dispensation, but she knew that such a marriage would be likely to leave Catherine, fairly soon, as the King's widow without being the mother of the King – a position wholly without influence. She offered Henry the widowed Queen of Naples instead, and urged again that Catherine be betrothed to Prince Henry.

King Henry answered by allowing the betrothal and backing it by a marriage-treaty rich in openings for future argument. He sent his ambassadors to investigate the Queen of Naples, armed with a questionnaire about her appearance.

Slow communications made it impossible for an ambassador to refer to his government once he had left home, so his instructions always contained detail of what to do in every possible contingency. In this case the questions about the Queen's person were in similar detail. They were to note her height, the favour of her visage, whether it were painted or not, and whether it were fat or lean, sharp or round, and whether her countenance were cheerful and amiable, frowning or melancholy, steadfast or light, or blushing in communication. Was her skin clear? What were her eyes, brows, teeth, lips, nose and forehead like? Were her arms fat or thin, long or short? What shape were her hands? How long was her neck? How big were her breasts? Had she any suggestion of a moustache? Had she got big feet? Was she a hearty feeder? What did she drink? All this was to be observed in the course of formal courtesies and conversation, during the course of which the ambassadors were to get close enough to find out 'the condition of her breath, whether it be sweet or not'.

Understandably, they had some difficulty in answering some of Henry's questions: 'At all times we have seen her Grace, ever she had a great mantle of cloth on her in such wise after the manner of that country that a man shall not lightly perceive anything except only the visage.' In kissing her hand they managed to establish that she had a pretty hand and a fairly large bosom, though it was 'trussed somewhat high' which might be deceptive. Her servants said she was a hearty eater and a temperate drinker. Her height seemed to be middling, but there was no way of knowing whether she wore high heels or no. As for her breath, craning forward in an attitude of reverence they sniffed and said that, all in all, she seemed to be 'of a sweet savour and well aired'.

But had she been a second Helen of Troy she had that about her which made the offer of her hand an insult: in her widowhood she had no reversion in Naples and no money except an allowance from Ferdinand. She could bring her husband neither money nor political influence. As the ambassadors returned home with this news Isabella of Castile died and her subjects began to plague English merchants in their ports.

Henry felt doubly cheated. He stopped Catherine's allowance, caused Prince Henry to make a formal protest against his betrothal to her, and started negotiations to marry himself, his son and his daughter into the family of Isabella's son-in-law, the Archduke Philip (whose wife Juana inherited Castile from her mother). The marriages foundered on the double obstacle of Philip's irresolution and his sister's unwillingness to be married to Henry. He paused to take breath.

While he was pausing the storm blew Philip and Juana ashore at Weymouth and led to the visit which settled the ending of Suffolk's wanderings. Juana's pale, melancholic beauty lingered in Henry's mind as she sailed away with her husband, and when he heard that Philip had died almost as soon as he reached Spain, he suggested that he marry her. Her being Queen of Castile and mother of the boy who would rule the Netherlands, all Spain and the Holy Roman Empire added to her attractions.

Juana herself proved an insuperable obstacle. All her married life she had been passionately, jealously devoted to her shallow, flighty husband. Now he was past all inconstancy, dead and in his coffin, hers alone. She set off on a second, macabre honeymoon, through the mountains of Granada, bell, book and miserere, refusing to have him buried. Her kingdom was nothing, affairs of state were nothing, second marriages could not even be thought of. Ferdinand stepped quietly into Castile and made hay while his daughter raved.

Henry – after questioning whether the lady was really insane or just eccentric, since her insanity seemed too convenient to Ferdinand to be credible – returned to haggling over Catherine's dowry. It was a long, discreditable battle between two professionals, neither of whom could bear to be bested by the other, and they ignored the fact that between them Catherine was penniless, pawning the plate which was part of her dowry to buy food. She pleaded with her father to send a really forceful ambassador to help her, and he sent one who prided himself on speaking his mind. Several interviews ended in Henry's losing his temper, and eventually the new ambassador was forbidden the court. Catherine's case seemed hopeless and she stayed on, with her unhappy, backbiting little entourage, only because she could not face Going Home to Father without having accomplished her mission in life – marriage to the future King of England.

It is commonly held that after the death of his Queen, Henry became increasingly curmudgeonly and rapacious, starving Catherine, hoarding money and exacting it unjustly from his groaning subjects. His evil reputation springs partly from our modern feeling that his varied proposals of remarriage were not quite nice – to his own generation such political moves seemed routine. The other sources of this feeling are the two major contemporary accounts of his reign – the *Chronicle of London* and the history written by Polydore Vergil, who came to England in 1502. They were both perhaps too close to the trees to see the wood clearly.

Henry recognised, before he became King, that the fall of the House of Lancaster had been caused not by divine wrath (see Shakespeare) but by insolvency (see English government of our own day). His whole reign was spent in establishing what were his fiscal rights and then exacting them. Naturally, wherever he was reclaiming rights unclaimed during the years of disorder, he was unpopular. He started with landowners, establishing which ones held their land directly from him and therefore owed him service and a form of death-duties. Sir Reginald Bray's department worked slowly and systematically, sometimes using methods which were dubious in equity, and by about 1500 most of Henry's rights on the land were established. Bray's department turned to the merchants. They began to enforce rigorously the penal statutes which governed trade and which laid down what penalty should be exacted in each case when a statute was broken. There being no police, they depended on private prosecutions by 'promoters' – informers – who were rewarded by receiving half the fine exacted in each case. Such a system was open to abuse and a number of promoters made these prosecutions their living (though none made a fortune from them). But all those people who had been getting away with it for a generation naturally felt a hot sense of grievance – as motorists do today if they are suddenly fined for speeding on roads where they have been doing so with impunity for years.

Polydore Vergil, arriving in 1502, got to know Bray, and developed a great admiration for him – Bray gave him most of the material for his history of the early years of the reign. Naturally Bray appears in a good light. When he died in 1503 his place was taken by other officials, notably Empson and Dudley, against whom there is a great mass of resentment recorded, but almost no concrete evidence of corruption. They seem to have been efficient and somewhat over-zealous, but that is all. Vergil recorded this unpopularity, but not that of Bray earlier in the reign – though the Cornish rebels in 1497 had been specifically after Bray's head.

It was three years before his death that Bray turned his attention to the merchants. Naturally, after applauding his dealings with landowners, they hated the new efficiency in dealing with traders, and naturally their reluctance was reflected by their own writer in the *Chronicle of London*. What seems to have happened is that Henry, through the course of his reign, became not increasingly rapacious but increasingly efficient.

Certainly he became increasingly isolated. He had never had the knack of winning popular affection, as his son and his grand-daughter Elizabeth would do. And in his last years there were few excuses for the splendid public spectacles which attended royal christenings and weddings, or the creation of royal dukes. There was no war, so no glory, and the memory of how expensive war was soon faded. The King could still be his old, engaging self – as he was with Philip and Juana in 1506 – but the occasion was lacking.

In fact, the reign had become safe, quiet and dull, and the English have always liked periodic changes of government. They came to take peace and prosperity a little for granted; to be impatient of the remote, cagey figure who had done so much to achieve prosperity and peace. Men long for rest, and are restless when they find it.

And for Henry also the excitement had gone. Many of those he loved most and those to whom he could open his heart and – equally important – his mind were gone. His life had been spent fighting and scheming and once the last Pretender was in the Tower there was almost no one left to fight or to outwit. There was only his son to watch, and the building at Westminster of a chapel designed to hold a tomb.

Foreign ambassadors had noticed from time to time that his health was failing. Early in 1509 he fell ill, as he often did in the spring, and on 21 April he died in the palace he had built at Richmond.

He had had the will to get and the skill to hold the shakiest crown in Europe, not by being an innovator or revolutionary, but by being more efficient, more industrious, more clear-sighted and determined than his opponents. Meticulous attention to detail and a cagey awareness of human weakness are unpopular virtues, and he was never able to capture the popular imagination – the crowds respected him in his majesty and gave their affection to his wife and children. But if he failed with crowds he succeeded with individuals: he chose his servants well and most of them served him long and faithfully. On a personal level he had charm and humour to counterbalance his reserve – the only Tudor to have what we should regard as a normal, stable family life.

'What he minded he compassed.' He took a weak throne and made it strong; he took his country's trade in a time of expansion and underpinned it with stable government and a strong currency; his diplomacy opened the door to Europe and the fresh wind blew in ideas at first invigorating and after his death such as would have appalled his medieval piety; he made the King's writ run in counties where for years the local landowner had been king, and set justice on a throne beside his own; he taught his people to associate peace and prosperity with the strength of the crown; he was a sportsman who loved the arts. He could be devious, relentless and ruthless, but he was one of the most perceptive, able and successful rulers this country has ever known.

By river to the City and St Paul's; by road from St Paul's to Westminster: he had a magnificent funeral. 'And then my Lord Treasurer and my Lord Steward did break their staves, and did cast them into the vault; and the other head officers did cast their staves in, all whole. Which done the vault was closed. And incontinent all the heralds did off their coat-armour, crying lamentably in French, "The noble King Henry the Seventh is dead".' Then they turned to the young man, eighteen years old, succeeding to a peaceful, prosperous kingdom, with more money in his coffers than any other ruler in Europe, ready to make a romantic marriage and to spend that money on music, games and glory. The future was young and exciting. 'And as soon as they had so done, every herald put on his coat-armour again, and cried with a loud voice, "Vive le noble Roy Henry le VIII"; which is to say in English tongue. "God send the noble King Henry the Eighth long life". Amen.'

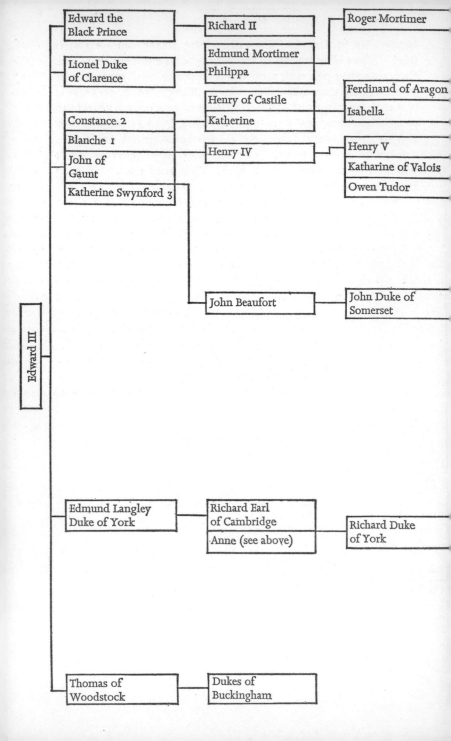

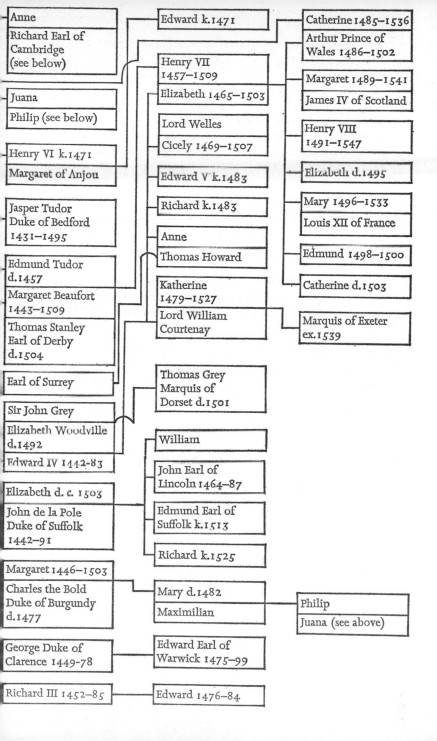

Anne / Richard Earl of Cambridge (see below)

Edward k.1471

Catherine 1485–1536 / Arthur Prince of Wales 1486–1502

Henry VII 1457–1509 / Elizabeth 1465–1503

Margaret 1489–1541 / James IV of Scotland

Juana / Philip (see below)

Lord Welles / Cicely 1469–1507

Henry VIII 1491–1547

Henry VI k.1471 / Margaret of Anjou

Edward V k.1483

Elizabeth d.1495

Richard k.1483

Mary 1496–1533 / Louis XII of France

Jasper Tudor Duke of Bedford 1431–1495

Anne / Thomas Howard

Edmund 1498–1500

Edmund Tudor d.1457 / Margaret Beaufort 1443–1509 / Thomas Stanley Earl of Derby d.1504

Katherine 1479–1527 / Lord William Courtenay

Catherine d.1503

Marquis of Exeter ex.1539

Earl of Surrey

Thomas Grey Marquis of Dorset d.1501

Sir John Grey / Elizabeth Woodville d.1492 / Edward IV 1442–83

William

John Earl of Lincoln 1464–87

Elizabeth d. c. 1503 / John de la Pole Duke of Suffolk 1442–91

Edmund Earl of Suffolk k.1513

Richard k.1525

Margaret 1446–1503 / Charles the Bold Duke of Burgundy d.1477

Mary d.1482 / Maximilian

Philip / Juana (see above)

George Duke of Clarence 1449–78

Edward Earl of Warwick 1475–99

Richard III 1452–85

Edward 1476–84

Chronology

1457   birth of Henry Tudor

1471   battle of Tewkesbury – Henry VI was captured and his son, Prince Edward, killed; Jasper Tudor took Henry and fled to Brittany

1474   birth of Perkin Warbeck

1475   birth of Edward, earl of Warwick

1482   death of Margaret Beaufort's second husband, Lord Stafford; Margaret Beaufort married Thomas, Lord Stanley, steward of Edward IV's household and member of his Council

1483   coronation of Richard III
the duke of Buckingham rose in favour of Henry Tudor and was executed
at Rennes cathedral, on Christmas Day, Henry proclaimed himself King of England and promised to marry Elizabeth of York

1484   Richard III's son died and the earl of Lincoln was proclaimed heir apparent
Henry fled from Brittany to France

1485   22 August – battle of Bosworth
30 October – coronation of Henry VII
7 November – opening of Parliament

1486   18 January – wedding of Henry VII and Elizabeth of York during the summer, Henry went on a progress to York, putting down risings headed by Lovell and the Stafford brothers. Lovell disappeared and the Staffords were taken from sanctuary to the Tower. Humphrey Stafford was executed
19 September – birth of Prince Arthur

1487   16 June – battle of Stoke
25 November – coronation of Queen Elizabeth

1489   January – the earl of Surrey was released from the Tower
27 March – treaty of Medina del Campo, allying England with Spain against France, and agreeing that Prince Arthur should marry Catherine of Aragon
28 April – murder of the earl of Northumberland; Surrey was sent north to replace him
Perkin Warbeck entered the service of Sir Edward Frampton
birth of Princess Margaret

1490   Prince Arthur became Prince of Wales

1491	the duke of Suffolk died and was succeeded by his son, Edmund de la Pole, as earl of Suffolk
	Perkin Warbeck travelled to Cork with Pregent Meno and John Taylor
	28 June – birth of Prince Henry
	6 December – Anne of Brittany married Charles VIII of France; the whole south coast of the channel was now in French hands
1492	Henry's finances moved into the black and stayed there for the rest of his reign
	Columbus discovered America
	Alexander VI (Borgia) became Pope
	Charles VIII invited Perkin Warbeck to France
	death of the dowager queen Elizabeth
	birth of Princess Elizabeth
	October – Henry invaded France and besieged Boulogne
	November – Treaty of Étaples between England and France, giving England an annual subsidy to keep out of France, and forcing Perkin Warbeck to move on – he took refuge with Margaret of Burgundy
1493	Maximilian became Holy Roman Emperor
	June – Sir Robert Clifford joined Perkin Warbeck
	September – the Flemish having refused to disown Warbeck, Henry broke off trade with Flanders
	November – Warbeck was received at Vienna with great honour by Maximilian
1494	Charles VIII invaded Italy
	Prince Henry became a knight of the Bath, Earl Marshal of England, Lord Lieutenant of Ireland, duke of York, and Warden of the Scottish marches
	Sir William Stanley, Sir William Mountford, Robert Ratcliffe, William Daubeney, Lord Fitzwater, the dean of St Paul's, the Provincial of the Black Friars and three other clerics were all arrested and charged with supporting Warbeck
1495	death of Jasper Tudor, duke of Bedford
	February – the Stanley conspirators were tried
	March – the Pope, Maximilian, Ferdinand, Venice and Milan formed the Holy League against France
	3 July – Warbeck failed to take Deal
	23 July–3 August – Warbeck besieged Waterford and failed to take it
	September – Warbeck was welcomed to Scotland, and James IV

rejected Henry's offer of a treaty and marriage with Princess Margaret

September – death of Princess Elizabeth

1496   Pregent Meno began to receive a pension from Henry

birth of Princess Mary

6 January – all foreign ambassadors to Maximilian met him at Nordlingen and insisted on his disowning Warbeck

24 February – Intercursus Magnus – the Archduke Philip abandoned Warbeck and Henry allowed trade with Flanders to start again

5 March – Henry granted John Cabot a licence to search for unknown lands beyond the 'eastern, western and northern seas'

14 March – Bernard de Vignolles confessed to the ointment plot

18 July – England was admitted to the Holy League without being bound to wage war on France

August – Princess Juana left Spain to marry the Archduke Philip

September – James IV and Warbeck raided Northern England

1497   Cabot reached Newfoundland

Juan, only son of Ferdinand and Isabella of Spain, died; their eldest daughter, Isabella, wife of the King of Portugal, became their heir

16 January – Henry's sixth Parliament opened; it voted taxes for war on Scotland and the taxation caused the Cornish rising

17 June – the Cornish rebels were defeated at Blackheath

August – betrothal of Arthur and Catherine, de Puebla standing in for Catherine

September – Warbeck captured in Cornwall

30 September – Treaty of Ayton, negotiated by Richard Fox, bishop of Durham, establishing a seven-year truce between England and Scotland; later in the year it was extended to a peace between Henry VII and James IV 'for the term of both their lives and either of them longest living, and a year after'

1498   birth of Prince Edmund

Isabella, Queen of Portugal, died, leaving her baby son heir to Spain and Portugal

Cabot went on his second expedition; he did not return

Vasco da Gama rounded the Cape of Good Hope

the royal palace of Sheen burnt down; it was rebuilt and its name changed to Richmond in honour of Henry's earldom before he became King

April – death of Charles VIII

June – Warbeck escaped and was recaptured and sent to the Tower during the Michaelmas term, the earl of Suffolk was indicted for manslaughter

1499   Wolsey became senior bursar at Oxford, and a fellow of Magdalen

Erasmus came to England, invited by young William Blount, lord Mountjoy; Thomas More took him to visit the royal nursery at Eltham

12 February – Ralph Wilford was hanged

1 July – the earl of Suffolk fled to Guisnes, to stay with Sir James Tyrrell

July – the French government, having captured John Taylor, handed him over to the English ambassadors, and he was sent to the Tower

Sir Robert Curzon, with Henry's permission, left the castle of Hammes and went crusading, stopping at Guisnes on the way to talk to the earl of Suffolk

4 August – contact was established between Warwick and Warbeck in the Tower

September – Sir Richard Guildford and Richard Hatton went to Guisnes and persuaded Suffolk to come home

Fox went to Scotland, charged with the negotiation of a marriage between James IV and Princess Margaret

October – Suffolk came home

November – Warwick, Warbeck and their followers were executed

1500   Ferdinand and Isabella's grandson died, leaving Princess Juana, wife of the Archduke Philip, as their heir

death of Morton, cardinal-archbishop of Canterbury

9 June – Henry and the Archduke Philip met near Calais

12 June – death of Prince Edmund

28 July – the Pope issued a dispensation allowing James IV and Princess Margaret to marry (they were fourth cousins by their common descent from John of Gaunt)

1501   Thomas Grey, marquis of Dorset, died

July – the earl of Suffolk and his brother, Richard de la Pole, fled to Maximilian

2 October – Catherine of Aragon reached England

14 November – Prince Arthur and Catherine were married

1502   January – James IV and Princess Margaret were betrothed

2 April – death of Prince Arthur

6 May – execution of Sir James Tyrrell

28 July – Treaty of Augsburg; Maximilian, in return for £10,000, promised to expel English rebels – having first made sure that Suffolk and his brother were safely in the independent city of Aix

1503 Sir Reginald Bray died

Pope Alexander VI died; Pius III reigned briefly and then Julius II became Pope

the Kentish conspiracies were hatching during the year

2 February – birth of Princess Catherine

11 February – death of the Queen, followed within a few days by that of Princess Catherine

25 June – Prince Henry and Catherine of Aragon were betrothed

27 June – Princess Margaret began her journey north

8 August – wedding of James IV and Princess Margaret

1504 negotiations for the marriage of Henry and the widowed Queen of Naples

death of Thomas, earl of Derby.

26 November – Isabella of Castile died

1505 27 June – Prince Henry made a formal protest against his projected marriage with Catherine of Aragon

1506 15 January – Philip and Juana, en route to claim Juana's inheritance of Castile, were driven ashore at Melcombe Regis in Dorset

9 February – Philip, at Windsor, agreed to surrender Suffolk to Henry

24 March – Suffolk reached the Tower

September – death of the Archduke Philip

1507 In the Michaelmas term Lord Bergavenny was fined for retaining 471 men for 30 months

1508 Sebastian Cabot sailed west and explored what may have been Hudson's Bay, returning after Henry's death

1509 21 April – death of Henry

11/71   WD